Training and Hunting
BIRD DOGS

Training and Hunting
BIRD DOGS

How to Become a Better Hunter and Dog Owner

SCOTT LINDEN

Illustrations by Constance Renfrow

Skyhorse Publishing

www.skyhorsepublishing.com

10 9 8 7 6 5 4 3 2 1

Library of Congress Cataloging-in-Publication Data

Linden, Scott.
    Training and hunting bird dogs: how to become a better hunter and dog owner / by Scott Linden.
          pages cm
    Includes bibliographical references and index.
      ISBN 978-1-5107-5593-2 (alk. paper)
1. Hunting dogs--Training. 2. Fowling. 3. Human-animal communication. I. Title.
      SF428.5.L54 2013
      636.75--dc23

ISBN: 978-1-5107-5593-2
Ebook ISBN: 978-1-62636-268-0

Printed in China

Contents

Foreword

"The more people I meet, the more I like my dogs."

—Ancient Roman graffiti

I BECAME A HUNTER after I watched my first German Wirehaired pointer work a field and put up a hen pheasant after a solid point. I'd never owned a gun, but I decided that if he would do that for me, the least I could do was shoot the bird for him. Little did I know this was going to be the start of a lifelong series of dazzling performances by a series of magical dogs I was privileged to observe. Though I started late in life, the relationship continues, and the awe I felt from that first point returns every time I send a dog into the field.

Any excuse for sharing time with a dog is legitimate, but for me, it is clear: we become a team linked by DNA, a modern version of a prehistoric wolf pack coursing the uplands for sustenance—literal and emotional.

In this digital age we pretend to communicate using gadgets. The talking we do at each other via smartphone is shallow, ephemeral, and self-centered compared to the deep genetic bond that exists between hunters. Words are unnecessary when instinct guides predators linked by common purpose.

I'm honored when my dogs invite me to share this primitive thrill, accepting me as their equal, calling on the most basic of instincts to feed our pack and sustain our souls. We are one, thinking and acting as a single being with a single goal: to find prey. The act is violent and primitive, ugly and beautiful, the most complicated transaction in the universe: Lives taking life to sustain life.

Neither of us will starve if we aren't successful in the common definition of the term. The size of our bag is a sidebar to a bigger story, i.e., the flow of adrenaline, deep passion, panting and slobber, the tang of sage, and, if we are lucky, the coppery smell of fresh blood.

Our dogs tolerate human missteps and bad shots. They put up with poor noses and slow, creaky joints in their human pack mate. At the end of the day they ask little except a warm place to sleep near their hunting companion, long past forgiving missed shots and misplaced anger.

We should be flattered.

Scott Linden
January 28, 2013

Introduction

IF YOU WATCH my television show you know I'm not a professional trainer, nor even a very good shot. I have a lot to learn about hunting too.

But I've been the companion of hundreds of dogs and their owners while making my show and for fun, and I am a pretty good observer, note-taker, and question asker.

Call me a dog "trainee" if you like, learning more from dogs than I could ever teach them. To better understand their lessons, I recorded many of them as I learned (and continue to learn). Many became blog posts, others magazine articles. They are presented here in somewhat chronological order so readers might better see the progression of skills.

Use this book as a supplement to your go-to training book or video. It will jump-start your hunting career and cram several years of learning into a season. It should shorten your learning curve, and if you're a seasoned hunter it might provide a few shortcuts and tips even you haven't thought of.

Look at it as having a very good friend who is an experienced bird hunter, one who is willing to share his knowledge with you all season. You'll condense the School of Hard Knocks into one reading instead of a decade of trial and error. As far as I can tell, the information isn't readily available anywhere else in books, on video or in seminars. I hope you find insights, observations, and ideas that will be helpful in your own hunting, shooting, and dog training.

See you in the field!

Acknowledgments

INEVITABLY WHEN ONE tries to thank every person who helped him compile a book of this sort someone is left out. I apologize in advance for that inevitability, and thank you for your kindness and assistance. You know who you are, even if I've been remiss.

While I doubt they will read this (they all went to school on athletic scholarships), thanks first to all the dogs I've hunted and trained with over the years. Each had something unique to offer me. My best teachers are my own wirehairs: Bill, Yankee, Buddy, and Manny. Guys, you are my inspiration.

Most dogs were kind enough to share their humans with me, and often they had as much to offer as their dogs. Thank you to the handlers, lodge operators, club members, trainers, and guides who spent time in the field, yard, and kennel with me.

Some humans had considerable impact on how I think about dogs. Thank you to George Quinlan, Bob Farris, Don Hewes, Ronnie Smith, and Larry Mueller.

Viewers, Facebook fans, and blog subscribers have come through like the family they are, offering ideas, suggestions, and feedback on everything from updating the Ultimate Upland Checklist to potential destinations for my show.

Thanks also to Jay Cassell at Skyhorse Publishing for having faith in this project. And thanks to my sponsors for their financial support of my *Wingshooting USA* television show, which made writing this book possible. Many are now good friends, particularly Dave Miles and Mark Thomas at the National Shooting Sports Foundation, Don Fenton and Al Chandler at TruckVault, Joe Exum at Happy Jack, Inc., Amy Terai and Harry Egler at Filson, Kurt Kaiser at Cabela's, and Terry Wilson at Ugly Dog Hunting Co.

Thanks also go to my hunting partners over the years, who have graciously shared their honey holes and put up with my bad shooting, lousy cooking, and overbearing company in chukar camp. Dave, this is for you.

Finally, thanks to my wife, Karen Dyanne Bandy, for putting up with my passion and frequent absences in pursuit of it. I hope you better understand now why I do it.

1

What Your Dog Wants

"If there are no dogs in Heaven, then when I die I want to go where they went."

—Will Rogers

DOGS ARE FASCINATING, multidimensional beings that have intrigued me for decades. The most interesting aspect of their lives, at least to me, is how they think. Maybe "think" is the wrong word for those who believe animals dwell deep in the primitive depths of instinct, fang, claw, action, and reaction, but we hunting dog owners know better. We've seen our partners apply reason, employ logic, solve complex problems, and learn a bit of "language." Sure, they think differently from us. But they think. And the sooner we figure out what they're thinking about—and why—the better our hunting team becomes.

Why He'll Work for You

Have you ever had a lousy boss? You know the type: harsh voice constantly berating you, cutting you down, badgering, yelling, and criticizing . . . never offering praise or encouragement.

Some of us have been lucky enough to have a good boss, or even been one. To others, it might have been a coach, teacher, scoutmaster, or neighbor. You remember them for their soothing demeanor, supportive attitude, mutual respect, and positive reinforcement. Heck, even their critiques were constructive, almost pleasurable.

Of the two, whom would you rather work for? For which would you gladly stay late to help with a rush order, or go the extra mile?

The same holds true for your dog.

I'm not saying you should curry favor, suck up, or kowtow to your pup. In the pack, your dog functions best when he understands the boundaries and knows who is in charge. In your house, yard, and field, that's always you. Establishing those boundaries and setting up your chain of command can be done in a number of ways, some better than others. One version engenders respect and cooperation; other versions foster fear or aggression.

When discipline is applied appropriately, instruction is melded with encouragement while correction is levied with restraint and sensitivity. I think your dog acquires a sense of "fairness." I doubt that dogs truly comprehend that term, but they are certainly aware of its opposite.

Doesn't it just make sense to create a relationship based on mutual trust, respect, and reward for a job well done? Remember when it worked for you? You can be sure it'll work for him as well.

So, What Does He Want?

Overtime pay, paid vacations, and bonuses are not high on your dog's list of priorities. But there is an evolving menu of rewards that may be used to

After all, he's a "bird dog."

encourage and compensate him for his good work. Withholding these rewards when appropriate results in just the opposite effect and becomes another useful strategy, so make a mental note of the two-way nature of this street.

There are a ton of things a dog loves, wants to happen to him or for him, wants to put in his mouth or roll in. Ironically, one in particular seems to be given short shrift in most training regimens. But it may be the most neglected and possibly most important reward your dog deserves.

He's a Bird Dog

Your dog lives, breathes, and sometimes eats birds. His entire reason for living is to pursue and capture birds. So what do we do the minute he brings us one? Snatch it away. To me, that doesn't make much sense.

Unless he's chomping or chewing, why not let him hold the bird for a moment once he sidles up to you on a retrieve? The intoxicating smell, taste, even the texture of feathers on tongue has got to be heaven for a bird dog. Why not let him savor it for a bit before sending him for the next one? In my kennel, a short "victory lap" around me while carrying the bird is okay too.

Just so he understands I'm not after his bird (at least for a bit), I'll often put my hands in my pockets, sit down, or turn my side to him while he's got a bird in his mouth . . . as long as he stays close. With a pup, stepping on his check cord will keep him nearby without your action being interpreted as stealing his bird.

Priority number two for my dog immediately becomes more birds. Sending him back to hunting instead of the kennel, truck, or walking at heel is another eagerly anticipated reward for bird dogs. For many retrievers it doesn't even have to be the real thing. "Fun bumpers" give them the same thrill.

A Little Handier

I think a dog would carry a hand-scrawled WILL WORK FOR FOOD sign if he had opposable thumbs. As predator-scavengers, a bird dog's next-highest priority is food. They are hardwired to swallow just about anything they can fit in their mouths, anything that resembles edible in the broadest sense of the term. (Maybe your dog, too, has gulped down socks, rocks, roadkill, and underwear.)

Commercial treats, bits of hot dog, even dry dog food are rewards that are easy to carry. Your peanut butter sandwich will do in a pinch. For training, I like portable, fingernail-sized pieces that won't stain my pockets or spoil too quickly. Soft foods are better than crunchy ones. Smaller, softer food rewards are chewed and swallowed quickly so your dog doesn't lose his train of thought and fall out of training mode crunching away at something more toothsome. Just make sure you know which foods are harmful to dogs. The list starts with chocolate and runs to raisins and onions, so do your research (check my first aid section).

On hot days, water is as welcome a reward as food treats.

Hot out there? Water works too. Teach your dog to drink from a Bota bag or bottle and you can share easily and somewhat hygienically. A bonus: you'll never lose the bowl or have to sacrifice your favorite hat.

Transcending Treats

As Shakespeare aptly pointed out, man does not live by bread alone. Neither does your dog. At some point, you'll need to advance beyond food treats for practical reasons, if nothing else. I don't always have a hot dog around, and I'll be darned if I'm giving up my last pretzel if there is still beer in the glass!

A good firm stroke makes both of you feel good.

Personally, I'm not grossed out by the next best thing: the residue left on my fingers after cleaning a bird. After all, dogs *are* scavengers! Some old-school trainers even proffer the head of the well-retrieved bird as a food treat.

Often it's the more personal touch, literally, that becomes the perfect pay-off after a stellar bit of dog work. A scratch behind the ear says, "Good job." Rubbing the pup's chest is welcomed by any dog, and most dogs will come right to you if they know you're going to offer more praise. And no dog can refuse a firm, slow stroke down his backbone. If he arches his back to meet your hand, you know you've provided the ultimate in physical rewards.

Perhaps more satisfying than a scratch or food treat is the sound of your voice. Tell your dog he's a good boy, over and over and over. Have a catchphrase if you need one, a secret language or nonsense word he knows means he's doing well. Be consistent with it—simple is better. Avoid using your dog's name—it has better uses, such as getting his attention prior to another command.

"Face time" is not just a business-speak cliché. A dog that can meet you face-to-face is a happy dog. As a puppy your dog licked his dam's face in the hopes of some regurgitated food. I'm not suggesting you go quite that far, but any dog will settle for the first half of the transaction. Anyone who doesn't let their dog lick their face once in a while probably prefers cats.

Sometimes, the best reward is the most subtle: simply being around you. This often works well as a discipline or correction tactic—withholding your attention by backing away from a gate will stop a dog's frantic circling, for example. Turning your back on a dog that's jumping on you will often halt it. Temporary banishment can be as effective as any shock collar.

Evolutionary biologists tell us the only reason dogs were domesticated, the sole reason they serve us, is because we've arrested their development. They contend (and I agree) that even adult dogs are in a state of perpetual puppyhood. They seek attention, positive reinforcement, and contact with the Alpha pack member in their lives, and that is us.

Yes, you do attract more flies with honey than with vinegar and the same holds true for your dog. I've made a practice of asking every pro trainer I meet how much praise he delivers compared to the number of corrections. It averages about seven rewards to every correction. As a rule, more (*much* more) praise is always the preferred approach.

A little demonstration you can try at home might help. (Thanks to trainer George Quinlan for putting me on the right track with this.) Ask another human to help by being the "dog." Now, imagine (but don't tell them) you've hidden a treat somewhere in the room and you want your "dog" to find it. In the first attempt, your communication is limited to "No" whenever your dog is moving the wrong way. In the second, you can only say "Good boy" when he's moving the right way. In the third, you can use both "No" and "Good boy." Which worked best for you both?

Praise for a job well done is not a release.

Finally, note that praise is not a release: "Good boy" can easily be miscon-strued by your dog as "Hunt on" without discipline on both your parts. Pause between praise and releasing him to resume hunting or before he's allowed to goof around, for that matter. Come up with a release word and be consistent about using it. Being permitted to resume hunting is reward enough for most dogs, but save yourself some aggravation by insisting he stand still until all the praise is delivered *and* a new command is issued.

Everything Is Relative

Think back to your own "training." Whether learning to ride a bike or use Facebook, someone was at your side, guiding, praising, correcting, and encour-aging. Early in the process it took a lot of feedback, positive and negative. Later, as you gradually mastered your task, not so much.

Depending on the skill and maturity of you, the student, the praise might have been effusive, loud, and frequent. As you matured, it might have been a subtle nod or single word. Ditto for constructive criticism. Your dog's unique personality and maturity will dictate how—and how much—praise or discipline he needs to become your best hunting partner.

I own two wirehairs: great uncle Buddy and grand nephew Manny. They may look alike and share much of their DNA, but Buddy is a "soft" dog, requir-ing kid-glove treatment, especially when being corrected. The poor guy takes it personally if he's within earshot when I discipline his nephew. Manny is a hardheaded, runaway freight train of a dog, often requiring a more aggressive approach. Now that I understand that, we get along just fine.

Summary: The Big Payoff

Food, water, a good scratch . . . they all work for the common goal. But let's not forget that our partner is a bird dog. It shouldn't take a rocket scientist to figure out the most effective reward. Without training, our very expensive predator-scavenger-partner would simply swallow that bird, maybe slowing down to deconstruct it first. With training, we can forestall such habits, still allowing our dog to savor the primordial reward of prey in his mouth.

It's the handler's job to provide this über-reward. Our dogs, in turn, will run five times as far as we walk, swim icy waters, endure cactus spines and sand burrs, shiver in brutal cold, and pant in searing heat. At the end of even the worst day they'll then curl up at our feet and sleep the sleep of the blessed.

I think it's a fair bargain. It's also what the rest of this book is about.

This is why he works for you.

2

How Your Dog Thinks . . . I Think!

"If you think dogs can't count, try putting three dog biscuits in your pocket and then give him only two of them."

—Phil Pastoret

JUST LIKE A therapist can best help someone by venturing inside their mind, we can guide our dog toward excellence by understanding how he thinks. This form of training is helpful primarily for us, adjusting the way we think based on how our dog reasons (or we *think* he reasons), rationalizes, and justifies his behavior.

We humans can think in more than one dimension. We plan ahead, reason, debate alternatives, and consider abstract concepts. Dogs, for the most part, string thoughts (actually, probably more like reactions than thoughts in the

Do we really know what comes next in his mind?

human sense) in a linear pattern. "A" is followed by "B," and then "C," and so on. If you work with phone company call centers often enough you may not always agree, but in general humans have much more experience with life—and learning—than the average dog does.

I've also noticed that dogs think literally. Here's the classic example: My dogs watch me enter the shop across the driveway from their yard. They spend much of the next half hour staring at the doorknob, willing it to redeliver me to them. I went in that way, I will come out that way (they think). If I exit from another door, they are baffled. A cruel variation is the hide-the-treat game, sneaking it from hand to hand behind your back. Again, they saw it in one hand . . . it must still be there, right?

Time and again I'm also reminded that dogs truly live in the moment. Their actions, desires and needs are *right now, right here*. Unlike the abstract thinking humans utilize (excepting some in-laws) canines are all about *now*. Look up "immediate gratification" in the dictionary and there will be a picture of a dog.

Mental Equals Physical

In addition to mentally moving one step at a time in what to them seems a logical order, dogs often also move physically in that fashion. Watch your dog complete some simple task. He'll likely take the shortest route between two points, unless there is an impenetrable (or more distracting) object between them. Because that object is a literal, physical obstacle, it can often put the kibosh on a dog's thought process and bugger up whatever you wanted him to do, i.e., retrieve a bird, come back to you, or go in his crate.

So how do you use this knowledge in a training situation? Thinking like a dog is a good start. Anticipate his next move (good or bad) and set up scenarios to ensure success based on the dog's literal and linear thought process.

Here's an example: Your dog scents a bird and points. Thanks to your superior mental abilities (Hah!) you have anticipated the menu of potential actions that might result. He could rush in and flush the bird on his own, or maintain his point, or slink away. You've been watching him carefully, so you are ready with a "Whoa" command the moment he screeches to a stop, front leg raised. You've restructured his linear thought process with your command and helped him to the next desired action—in this case, a staunch point. You've circumvented his instinctive desire to crash in and catch the bird, guiding him to a much better (in your eyes) outcome.

Knowing these traits can help in how you give direction, teach a skill, or establish reasonable expectations for your dog at whatever stage or age they have reached.

Anticipate

Like any good Boy Scout, I prefer to be prepared when I give my dog a command. If possible, I wait to call my dog to me when there is nothing blocking his route. Trees, shrubs, people, noise, and other dogs all increase the chance of distraction and his losing track of the original command and destination. The same goes for retrieves—a straight route is the least distract-

No obstacles between a young Buddy and me ensure compliance to the "Here" command.

ing. Want him to power into his crate at night? Get everything out of the way first. Even another human making eye contact can cause Fido to veer off course. As they progress and you want to challenge them, add physical as well as mental distractions to keep them on their toes.

Likewise, it helps in the early stages of training to go with the flow. A dog that is running in your direction is a good candidate for a "Come" command. With young dogs, that's exactly when *not* to deliver a "Whoa." Conversely, your odds of getting a half-trained dog that is racing away from you to reverse field and "Come" are pretty sketchy.

Does their different way of thinking mean we should dumb down their training? That wouldn't be my choice of words. Rather, put yourself in his place, try to imagine what he is seeing, reacting to, and anticipating, and then direct and correct accordingly. If you watch your dog carefully, you can often preempt him from doing bad stuff, and then you can guide him to do good stuff simply by better understanding his thought process.

Sometimes Smarter

Every once in a while, I'm reminded that we are occasionally smarter than our dogs. Using that slight mental advantage when training can prove invaluable. I'll use sleight of hand to keep my dogs on their toes—surprised, ready for anything. Or, my goal may be to simply break up the routine to avoid getting stuck in a rut. Either way, they are thinking, situationally aware, and paying attention. And those are good things. See if these magic acts work for you and your dog.

Dogs that jump up probably have a good reason. Often I've got a bowl of food in my hand. I want Buddy to walk alongside me, bowl en route, to his crate where he eats as I deliver his bowl, but his walking is more like a series of hops as he does his scavenging best to get at the food before we get to the crate.

Yesterday I switched hands, putting my body between bowl and dog so that the food was out of sight. I got a nice, polite walk at heel all the way to the crate. It was not as flashy as a rabbit out of a hat, but it worked.

Sometimes at the glimpse of a training bird, a fired-up pup can't contain himself and begins spinning, jumping, and whining out of control. When this happens I keep the bird well hidden until I can spring it upon my unsuspecting dog. The shock factor is often enough to freeze him in his tracks, often eliciting a point.

I can think of a number of ways to outsmart a dog at least some of the time. Hiding from a pup in the field encourages him to remain aware of your location. Put two planted birds in the same spot, and then flushing one while the dog points the other could help him hold steady through the first bird's flight.

Surreptitiously dropping a bird while out walking, and then asking your dog to "Hunt dead," often gets the drop on him too. Even walking to a shot bird to pick it up yourself rather than bidding your dog to retrieve it could be considered a trick.

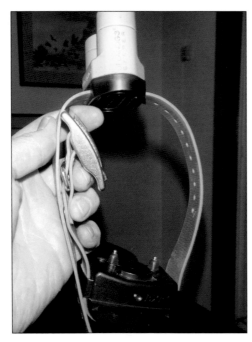

To my dogs, this means an adrenaline rush.

Hiding food treats so their provision is an unexpected surprise is almost a Magic 101-level trick, but it works. But don't torment your trainee. If you normally praise your dog with food treats, be up front when you're not using them. I show my empty hands to my dogs before I ask them to do something for which they are accustomed to getting a tidbit.

My dogs get an adrenaline rush when they see me carrying their electronic collars. They often wiggle so much I can barely get the collars on them! So, I'll hide the collars in my vest, give them sixty seconds of unbound joy outside the gate, and then call each in turn, slipping their collars on without all the drama that went on just a minute ago.

The list goes on and on. Think about how you need to dial down, change up, or otherwise alter the status quo with your dog. A magic trick up your sleeve might be just what you need.

Emotion, Angst, and Anxiety

Like people, dogs can become nervous and anxious, curious, or protective. Think of the greeting you get when you pull into the driveway: dogs barking, jumping at the gate, running in circles. At our house, lace on a pair of boots and everyone gets amped up higher than an electronic collar set on six!

Lots of us try to stop high-energy behavior with yelling or high-energy discipline, but that only propels the stress level toward the stratosphere because we are essentially fighting fire (high anxiety) with fire (louder, more aggressive, more stressful).

This is probably not a good time to expect obedience to a command.

Fight Fire with Water

I'm a type-A kind of guy but am slowly learning that staying cool and calm is a better way to interact with my hyperactive dogs. I'm doing my best to anticipate stress-inducers, heading them off before they impact my dogs' behavior, calming them by maintaining my own cool head and actions.

My older dog Buddy is a mirror of my emotional state, so responsive to my internal machinations you'd think we were linked telepathically. When he is nervous or tentative I know it's probably something I'm doing. Conversely, he has shown me how to stay positive, avoid these issues, and get back to hunting or training . . . with distraction and diversion. He's taught me to dial down my own energy level.

It can sometimes be as simple as breaking his train of thought. Calling his name, a hand clap, hitting the locator beeper, or offering a food treat might solve the immediate problem. If the behavior persists, you're going to have to get out of your recliner.

Leaving the house can lead to separation anxiety. That in turn can lead to new curtain purchases, expensive carpet cleaning bills, and long explanations to the sheriff's deputy when the neighbors complain about incessant barking. If your dog really suffers when you are gone, you'll want professional advice. But in the short term, ask someone to help by training or playing with your dog as you're heading out the door for work. I try to keep things low key when departing and returning, even sneaking away if necessary.

Even when you're home, barking can drive you and your neighbors nuts. Why not shift the dynamic, and distract your hunting partner with something more productive? A retrieving session shifts his mental state to a more constructive mode, as might a few obedience drills.

Dial down an anxious situation with something positive, such as a retrieving drill.

At our house, deer are the main distraction for our dogs—we have a bunch living behind the place. At your house, it might be other dogs, the mail carrier, or passing cars. All of these can be a source of interest—and anxiety—to a dog.

Whether it's a porcupine or a rival stud, you're better off being proactive with something more engaging than having to break up a confrontation. Have a go-to strategy and keep it handy: a retrieving bumper by the front door or a command for something he'll drop everything to do. I like "Dinner time!"

Unless you've got the perfect dog, you and he can both use a little more training. Any diversion from bad behavior is like hitting two birds with one shot.

Breaking Boredom

Do dogs get bored? Boy howdy, do they! Howling, digging, fighting, and barking are all indicators of a dog with too much mental free time. But boredom isn't limited to lying around in the yard, waiting for the paperboy to ride by. A dog that backslides on his training may be like the underachiever in class: he needs more challenges than his teacher is giving him.

Time and again I've watched my dogs go off the rails as if we'd never worked on retrieving, "Whoa," or simple obedience skills. Usually it's me who's

gotten stuck in a rut—too much repetition of the same skills at the same level that we both end up phoning it in.

Back to the class underachiever. Your dog may resort to canine spitballs, resisting your commands, or worse if you aren't fully engaging his mind. And all of a sudden, you're back to square one on skills you'd thought were mastered.

Of course there is risk in raising the bar. Dogs that are asked to go too far, too soon beyond their abilities may fail. Whenever possible you want to avoid that. But it's occasionally worth the risk—when you

Raise the bar for a bored dog with something new to retrieve.

see him losing interest—to help your dog reach for the stars.

Example: We were working on the NAVHDA (North American Versatile Hunting Dog Association) Utility-level "duck search." Ultimately, Manny would be required to swim and wade a brushy pond for ten minutes, trying to find a wing-shackled duck that is doing its best not to be found. The most valuable skill for the dog in this test is using his nose to sniff out the faint duck scent that lingers in the air and on the water, sometimes even on the water plants. It's easy for Manny entering a small pond downwind of the duck—that's his comfort zone at this time. But every once in a while, I'll put him on the upwind side of the pond so he has to expand his search before hitting the duck scent.

There are any number of ways to take it up a notch with your dog. Has he mastered retrieving from the "Whoa" table? Go somewhere else, or have him fetch something different. Working on "Heel"? Have someone—or someone with a dog on a leash—stand nearby while you reinforce your command. The simplest way to up the ante is to practice previously mastered skills in new locations or with added distractions.

In field skills, often the challenge becomes proximity. My young dog holds a point well when birds flush at a distance of fifteen feet or more. Obviously, putting dog and bird closer together increases the challenge to the point it

The ultimate goal, but it starts far, far away.

might require a firmer hand. But eventually your dog will rise to the challenge if you've prepared him, one baby step at a time.

Make a list of skills you think you and your dog have down pat. Then add another column with ways to make the same tasks harder—in increments—and you'll keep your dog firing on all eight cylinders.

Give 'Em a Break

Mondays may not be your favorite day of the week, but if you rested Saturday and Sunday you will be refreshed, reinvigorated, and ready to face the work week. Conversely, if you worked all weekend you're probably not at the top of your game when you clock in again on Monday morning.

Dogs are the same. They need a break from training once in a while. There's only so much undivided attention I can expect. So I give them a "weekend" off here and there too.

Some days, we just play, explore new places, or hunt. We go back to the easy stuff on the training agenda or practice old skills in new places. What we don't do is focus on acquiring new skills until the old ones have been mastered.

After a few days of introductory work, I let the newest bits of knowledge sink in, so to speak, without continuing to train, which can burn the dog out.

A welcome break from a few days of hard training.

This way dogs—and their handlers—enjoy a no-stress holiday that makes the next intense training session more productive.

It's kind of like when we put on our sweatpants and watch football all day. We still know where the fridge is and how to open it, but it is second nature and doesn't require much concentration—that is, until we can't figure out where our wife hid the beer!

Be Honest with Your Dog

Neither of my dogs has a conniving bone in his wiry, hairy body. But humans are predisposed to use guile, wit, and cunning to get what they want. It is tough sometimes, but I try to be honest, at least with my dogs and spouse. Trust is a two-way street and it starts with a dog having confidence in you in your interactions with him. Knowing how he thinks, I can help manage his expectations and deliver what he expects.

Remember the fable of the boy who cried wolf? If your deceptive actions teach your dog not to believe what you're saying or doing, you've eroded that underpinning of trust that is critical to a strong working partnership. If you ask your dog to retrieve a bird, make sure there's one out there for him. Shoot well and always mark your downed birds. In training, bring an extra bird just in case. In a rare case of brilliance, I lobbed a dead ringneck for a hardworking young

Going on sixteen months old, he doesn't need a food treat for every good retrieve anymore.

shorthair when my partner whiffed on a flushing bird. Duke didn't know the difference and was rewarded with the ultimate treat—a bird in his mouth.

If he's expecting a reward, don't withhold it when the job's done right. The other side of that coin is, don't give a command you can't enforce. Enforce and correct every time you deliver a command or your dog will wonder when you're serious and when you're crying wolf. It may be funny—to you—but pulling tricks (like hiding his food treat from him) only teaches him you can't be trusted.

An honest relationship is easier to maintain if you are consistent: same words, same tone, same expectations every time.

Correction is a tough row to hoe. Until your dog truly understands the command you're teaching, punishment (however you define it) is out. Helping him physically or mentally to do the right thing is in. Hitting a dog is the ultimate betrayal. It's the canine equivalent of biting the hand that feeds you. A dog should trust your hands—they deliver food, physical praise, even first aid. If they also deliver a blow, you're sending a mixed message.

In the field, you put all your trust in the dog. He'll return the favor if you've built your relationship on a firm foundation of honesty.

3

Communicating
with Your Dog

"If a dog will not come to you after having looked you in the face, you should go home and examine your conscience."

—Woodrow Wilson

IN THE CLASSIC movie *Cool Hand Luke*, there's a pivotal scene where the sneering, brutal prison warden says to Paul Newman's character, "What we have here is a failure to communicate." It's a prime example of neither party getting what it wants simply because they can't—or don't want to—make their respective points clearly.

When it comes to your dog, being clear and concise is critical to success. If your dog understands precisely what you want from him, he will be more likely to perform well in the field, in the yard, and in your home. And, if you know what your dog needs, you can help him better understand you.

Revise Your Lexicon

I give seminars and talks at events all over the country, and a recent session at a local Pheasant Fest generated some spirited feedback and fascinating stories of other dog owners' trials, tribulations, and triumphs. The most intriguing discussion in the aisle had to do with which words to use for which commands, and why.

In my mind simple is better. According to the US Army, your pup could conceivably understand over 200 different commands. Not at my house! I give my dogs easy-to-yell names . . . one or two syllables. That way, they learn their unique signal faster.

Furthermore, soundalike commands are a major bugaboo. Many of our *commands* can sound like *names.* Name your setter "Beau" and he might "Whoa" when you want him to hunt on. "Rover" sounds like "Over," a common command among retriever handlers. And "No" sounds like "Beau" or "Whoa," adding to the confusion.

I strive for distinctive words for each desired action. Momma dog uses "Aagh!" when she disapproves of a new pup's actions. Why not take advantage of genetics and use it too? (It may be academic. At our house, most dogs' first names end up being "Goddammit," at least early in their careers.)

"Here" is easier to yell than "Come." But "Heel" and "Here" sound the same, so my "Heel" command is "Walk." I don't use "Over" when I want my dog to change direction, I use "Way" as the command, often accompanied by a hand signal. My release command can't be "Okay," or there'll be more confusion: the dog may think I'm asking him to hold still . . . as in "Stay." "All right" is safe and sounds like nothing else in the lexicon.

I have a theory that most dogs simply hear the vowel and ignore the consonants. Testing this theory on Buddy probably doesn't prove much other than I'm a bad trainer, but it seems to ring true. At Pheasant Fest, one of my new friends disputes this theory and offers various command words and tricky situations where he has tested his dogs and they have learned the difference. More power to ya, Andy. But as I said, for me and Buddy at least, simple is better.

Keep It Simple

The Dave Barry cartoon where poor Ginger the dog hears, "Blah, blah, blah, Ginger, blah, blah, blah" is closer to the truth than most dog owners realize. Remember, dogs think in a linear manner. Stringing a long line of words together requires a long thought process, something dogs are less capable of than we humans are (Packer fans notwithstanding). Consider developing a shorter training vocabulary. Keep out extraneous words. Think Hemingway, not Shakespeare. Leave the expansive narrative for the post-hunt campfire story. Your hunting buddies may be better at the long thought process than your dog, but I'll let you be the judge.

Moving Things Along

Dogs are sort of color blind. The anatomy of their eyes is different than ours, so they see yellow and blue, but no red as we do. Why? Canine eyes have fewer cone cells than we do, according to veterinary ophthalmologists. There is an upside; dog eyes have more rod cells than our eyes, enabling a dog to see more clearly than we do in low-light conditions.

Those same sort-of color-blind eyes are superior in another way: They are built to detect moving objects more quickly. It's logical. Moving things equal prey. Motionless things are usually inedible. In the wild, a canid that can't tell the dif-

The added distraction of a cameraman on the ground only reinforces the need to be creative with hand signals.

ference could starve. You've probably seen this phenomenon at work. Dog, dozing in the yard. Squirrel, nibbling an acorn. All is quiet. Squirrel finishes his snack and scampers for a tree. Dog chases. (Of course, scent is a different story, as we shall see!)

Knowing this, why not use motion to better communicate with your dog?

Probably by accident, I found that hailing my dogs from a distance with a raised hand was useful. But waving it back and forth produced much better results. When I shared this revelation with a trainer friend of mine, he offered his own success story. Young dogs retrieve to hand better when that hand is opening and closing. The dogs power toward him, perhaps thinking he has a bigger bird in his hand than they do in their mouths!

Watch a retriever trainer and you'll probably see him throw an imaginary ball in the direction he wants his dog to go. An eager Lab, sitting enthralled, follows his arm, does an about face, and streaks down a line behind him where (he thinks) a dead duck awaits his retrieve. While training a young dog to "Come," you'll often have success if you pretend to run away from him.

When I'm training to a marked retrieve, I'll put my hand, karate-chop style, in my dog's line of sight while pointing at the dead bird. Just before I send him, I'll give my fingers a little wiggle to make sure he's looking straight down that line.

In the field, when I'm asking my dog to move left or right with arm signals, I'll often start with my arm overhead, then arc it down to point in the direction I want him to go. Or, I'll use "jazz hands"—wide open, fingers spread, and then wiggle the whole hand a bit. Sounds silly, but it works. After all, we're looking for lines of simple, clear communication between you and your dog, not rehearsing to be on *Dancing with the Stars*.

Timing Is Everything

Elsewhere I talk about "tells," those little signs that indicate that your dog is getting birdy or ready for direction or in need of correction. We'll also talk later about timing your commands, praise, and correction for that "golden moment" when he's amenable to them. But just like those indicators of readiness, there are times when you're wasting your breath and your emotional energy. You can yell, scream, jump up and down, do cartwheels, and throw your whistle, but your dog will steadfastly ignore you.

It think it was Delmar Smith, legendary professional dog trainer, who said, "Never give a dog a chance to fail." I take that to mean don't expend training capital—or sanity—giving commands that are destined to be ignored. The dog still learns, but not what you hoped to teach. He learns he can get away with murder.

As a dog matures and training progresses, he will be more likely to listen to you and pay less attention to the siren song of distant roadkill. It is a gradual and cumulative process, so keep your expectations at an appropriate level.

What kind of clues should inspire you to stow your whistle? Some are obvious. My dog Buddy is a digger. When he's bored and there are no birds he's happy enough hunting ground squirrels. Once he's digging, there is no point in my asking, telling, imploring, or threatening. He's in predator mode, single-minded and focused on the critter that is frantically tunneling away at warp speed.

Virtually any distraction has the same effect on a dog's brain. They are linear thinkers after all, one idea at a time. Run. Stop. Pee. Run. Smell critter. Run toward it. There's no room for other thoughts during this process, so don't try to intervene. A dog in hot pursuit of a whitetail is not going to "Whoa" until he's good and ready to do so.

The perfect time to deliver a command.

Distractions, such as other dogs, people, and sounds, can confuse a dog and flummox a command. When this happens, breathe deep, give it a minute, wait for your opportunity, and then deliver your directive when there's an open niche in the thought process. Right after he pees and before his hiked leg hits the ground is a perfect time. Following a good shake is another. While he's howling at a neighbor jogging past is not the most opportune moment.

Hunger or anticipation of a meal is another deal breaker. Once a week I catch myself wondering why Manny won't listen, let alone follow my clear direction. Then I look at the wall clock—it's dinner time.

Occasionally, something in the wind will entice the dog, and it doesn't need to be bird scent. Dogs often react first to what their noses tell them. If you don't give that new scent a beat or two to sink in, your command will fall on deaf canine ears. If you don't catch him before that initial shoulder tuck, you probably won't forestall a roll in that stinky dead critter he's found.

Their minds are on food, not your directions.

With a dog, learning is a gradual progression of baby steps, slowly leading to mastery of commands to the point of flawless obedience in the face of compelling distractions. The yin of your direction is constantly buoyed by the yang of sweet temptation. Only with repetition and gradual introduction of distractions can you tilt the balance in your favor. Even then, there's always a chance that you will lose out to roadkill.

Clarity of Hand

Voice and whistle are the lingua franca of human-canine communication. It may be prudent to consider teaching your dog via hand signals unless you want to sound like Rod Stewart during a particularly bad hunt. Save your sanity by using your hands in concert with your head. Just avoid using hand movements that could confuse your dog, especially if your dog was held back (twice) at obedience school, as was my wirehair Buddy.

Never give a signal with your left hand while your right hand is sticking out. To a dog this is the same as mumbling. Watch your shotgun, too, because from a distance, a gun barrel looks like an arm, and you could be sending mixed messages to an otherwise savvy bird dog. Put your extra hand in your pocket if you need to.

Because I like to keep things simple, and surely Buddy does as well, we get along better when I do things his way. In large part that means eliminating hidden obstacles that may result in a failure to communicate with my hands as well as my voice.

Which way will he go?

Consider the Dog's Point of View

Last year, I rigged a high-definition video camera on Buddy and put him through his paces. Later, I played back the video. Pardon the pun, but it was an eye opener. Now that I know what my dogs see, I will be more specific about what I want them to do and add audible clues to most of my hand signals.

Being all of twenty inches off the ground, Buddy can seldom see me as well as I can see him. It's a simple matter of geometry—the angle of his eyesight ends at every bush, tree trunk, and hummock between him and me. When I'm signaling him to change directions, the brush often obscures most of my body, not just my hand. No wonder he ignores me half the time!

In heavy cover an arm held to my side to signify "Over" can be lost behind a tree trunk. My beckoning open palm is hidden by a bush. Even when I can see his whole body, if I can't see his eyes there's a good chance he can't see the business end of my arm and the signals I'm giving.

Next time you're in the field, think about what you learned in your last geometry class, especially when you're giving hand signals.

The Eyes Have It

The eyes have been said to be the window to the soul, but they are also the portal to your dog's understanding of commands. Dogs are great readers of body language, so while your voice is giving the command and his ears may be hearing it, his eyes are searching—for what, I'm not sure, but definitely something. I believe your

Tall cover; this arm signal won't be seen by a short dog.

No wonder Buddy looks confused—who's behind the sunglasses?

dog needs to see your eyes to complete the transaction. Cover them with dark glasses and he is less likely to respond to your commands.

I don't know if my dogs simply don't recognize me, can't trust me because there's no "face" to match my voice, think I'm a space alien, giant bug, or what, but I do know that dark glasses muck up the communication process. While you ponder this, also consider beards and unusual hats. I've seen these and other subtle changes in the handler's appearance cause conniption fits in some dogs too.

Face It

Some people say I have a face for radio, not television. But my dogs know that my face can help them become a better hunter. They may be *my* face's only fans!

Bird dogs key on your body's most visible, brightest component and try to keep it in sight. Well-bred hunting dogs will try to stay in front of you, and they know it's the front because they can see your face. How can you use this to your advantage in the field?

Sometimes, all you have to do is look in the direction you want your dog to go. A cooperative dog will try to put your face behind him. Want him to change course? Just turn and face in that direction.

When you need a strong, independent, creative "Hunt dead" retrieve, direct him to the proper spot with your face, not by walking around in the brush. This will keep your scent out of the area, but still puts him where the bird fell. Some hunt tests require the handler to be silent during portions of field, water, and retrieving work. Or, you may not want to spook other birds in the field. Be quiet and let your face do the talking.

When your dog needs direction your face can be a shining beacon. He may not have a very refined aesthetic sense, but to your dog your face may be the best thing he's seen all day.

It's a Cacophony Out There

Next time your dog disobeys you, don't jump to obvious conclusions: It may not be recalcitrance. He may not be stubborn. There's a chance he's not even disobeying. He simply may not be able to hear your commands.

When I attached that video camera to Buddy last season, it was clear from the playback that there are vision challenges when looking to a tall human for direction. Thanks to the microphone on that camera, I've learned that it's an audio circus down there too.

Depending on whom you believe, dogs hear up to ten times better than us. It may even be much more than that. So, many of the annoying little pops and crackles we hear sound like a freeway accident to him. Think about what he encounters down there: tags jingling from his collar, brush crashing, screeching wind, footfalls on dry leaves, maybe a beeper collar right behind his ears, his own panting. All are overwhelming those frantic commands being yelled into that auditory chaos.

Your Lab's ears may be hammered by a flock of Canada geese honking or the churn of moving water as he looks to you for a line. Maybe there's another whining dog in the blind, or at a hunt test there could be dozens of barking dogs staked out nearby. It's no wonder hunting dogs bungle their job once in a while. It could be that they can't hear our commands for all the chaos at ground level.

If there's doubt in your mind about whether your dog can hear you, be sure to include hand signals or a whistle in your training, just in case. Call his name and wait for acknowledgment before giving a command. Just remember that when an experienced dog fails to respond, there's probably a good reason for it. Try to cut your dog some slack.

This might make it hard to hear commands.

4

Shooting Better

"When you have shot one bird flying you have shot all birds flying. They are all different and they fly in different ways but the sensation is the same and the last one is as good as the first."

—Ernest Hemingway, *Winner Take Nothing*

IF NO FEATHERS fly after a tail-stiffening point, you've disappointed your dog to no end. Once he's locked up, how do you ensure you'll actually hit something? Pay attention to him and your surroundings, and eliminate as many variables as possible. You'll be putting the odds in your favor.

Being aware of your dog might make you a better shooter.

Lock Him Up

I was recently reminded of how working with our dogs, thinking like they think, can result in better shooting performance from us. In South Dakota, a companion became so nervous (or was he dazzled at Buddy's stellar performance?) the bird had plenty of time to fly wild or scoot out from under Buddy's point. The hesitant hunter snuck, skulked, minced, and tiptoed over 100 yards—it seemed to take eons for him to flush that danged bird!

The rest of us were going batty, urging him to step on it. I was hoarse from yelling across the stubble. Luckily, the bird held and the outcome was favorable for the hunter. Here's the lesson:

First, ensure a solid point so that a bird holds still rather than scampering off unscathed. Start by being punctual. Once your dog stands the bird, walk in with vigor. The longer you dawdle, pausing to admire the dog's stunning good looks, or stop to take photos, the greater the chance that the bird will flush wild or run off. Or, the impatient dog will do the flushing for you.

Assert yourself. Over many years in many fields one thing has become clear: both birds and dogs hold better when the gunner moves in with confidence. Once your dog shows you the bird, stride briskly to the bird and everyone will likely do what's expected of them. This is the time to show you are in charge. Be confident, but choose your route with care. When approaching pointed birds, swing wide around the dog and you'll effectively eliminate one of the bird's escape routes. Two gunners performing a pincer movement means fewer bolt-holes for a cunning rooster, which is often more inclined to sprint than fly. If you can put the bird between you and the dog there's a good chance it will fly, not run.

Moving in with confidence can staunch up a dog—and a bird.

Your approach can help—or hurt.

Flanking your dog also minimizes his likelihood of breaking point. "Allelo-mimetic behavior" is a highfalutin term to describe that flock of birds that jinks in unison, or a pair of wolves on the hunt, trotting along in parallel. Sauntering close alongside a pointing dog is an invitation to follow you into the flush—that's how we teach "Heel," after all.

"Stand" by for Birds

Okay, so the dog is staunch on point, muscles quivering, eyes bulging. He's done his part and so far you haven't bollixed things with your clumsy approach. The bird is still somewhere under that bush, right? Now let's do our darndest to hit it when we pull the trigger.

The good clay target shooters anticipate a bird's trajectory and set their feet for it. I'm no slouch when it comes to stealing great ideas, and neither are you, right? With a little knowledge and experience, you can probably make an educated guess as to which direction that rooster will launch itself. That information will help as you approach and, ultimately, how you set your feet for the shot.

This sporting clays shooter set his feet where he expected to hit the target . . . and he did. Bird hunters can too.

As you move in to flush your quarry, anchor your "off" foot (left if you shoot right-handed) pointing in about the direction you hope the bird will fly. If you're flushing the bird yourself save that last step and make it in the direction you anticipate the bird will fly.

Your other foot should be nicely squared off for balance (not too far behind your left foot), with both feet about shoulder width apart. This stance provides the maximum arc when you swivel your hips—quite helpful on fast-moving bobwhites, for example.

Are you ready to flush the bird? Almost!

The Head Game

Once your dog finds a bird, it's time to get your head in the game, literally—but not your hat. Push your cap brim high on your forehead or you'll raise your cheek off the stock to see the bird when you shoot. You will undoubtedly miss as a result.

Reconnoiter the area as you approach your dog so there's a better chance your feet and shotgun will be pointed in the proper direction when the bird comes up

on whirring wings. Flushed game birds often head for a ridge, point, or nearby high spot, instinctively trying to put that topographical barrier between them and the danger you pose. In their absence even ground dwellers like chukars might bolt for the cover of trees or tall shrubs.

Nice cap, but the bill obscures my sight picture.

Focus like he does.

On point, Buddy is totally focused on the bird as if he has blinders on, locked in with eyes like laser beams. It's a relentless gaze that says, "Gotcha." You should develop the same mindset too. Shooting instructor Buzz Fawcett calls it shooting like a predator, a physical and mental single-mindedness that eliminates distractions and puts birds on the ground for the dog. Here's how it works:

Keep *your* eye on the *bird's* eye as it flies. Focus completely. Once the bird flies, *see* it, don't just look at it. Keep your face on the gunstock, maintaining an accurate sight picture until the bird tumbles. Ignore your friends, the dog, other birds in a covey. Focus solely on the bird you are going to kill. Once you pull the trigger, watch it fall but keep your shotgun to your shoulder. This will keep your cheek on the comb of the stock where it belongs, ensuring good follow through.

Eliminate the Variables

I'm always looking for fresh excuses for my poor wing shooting: I tripped over a rock, bird flew out of its scent . . . and my go-to defense: the moon got in my eyes. Fair warning—you've read this far, so that one is now off the table.

Ideally, "bad gun mount" should also be banished from the lexicon of excuses. To do

Little movement is required to mount and shoot.

this, bring your gun to the "ready" position for the last few steps as you move to flush the bird. Bring the buttstock into your armpit, muzzle at about the height you expect to begin your gun swing. Try to swing from below the bird, pulling the trigger as the gun muzzle passes through the target. Put your lead hand far enough out on the forearm to enable you to push the gun forward and then back into the cup created by your shoulder with minimal up-down movement of the muzzle. To most of us, this means "choking up," bringing that hand a bit closer to the receiver and our body. Use your trigger hand only to pull the trigger. It shouldn't be carrying much of the gun weight as you mount it, or you'll get an up-down swivel that leads to missed shots.

One Bird at a Time

If I want Manny's full attention and undying devotion, I remember that one bird in the bag is worth two in the air. Too often when I try too hard for a double the result is two clean misses. I raise my head off the stock to watch the first bird fall, or don't swing through, or start looking for the second bird before I've shot the first.

As we now know, our dogs think linearly, and in shooting so should we. Shoot the first bird first, see it drop, mark it carefully. Only then, and if you have time, should you contemplate a second shot. But make sure the first bird is dead and down where you can quickly find it.

Need another reason to hold off? On covey birds, always expect a late riser, a lingering bird that will often flush long after the smoke—and your mind—have cleared. Save your second barrel for him, and your friends will soon be buying the first round at the end of the day.

Open Your Pattern

In the days of silk fly lines, English fly anglers would utter, "God save the Queen" before setting the hook. This gave the trout time to take the fly in his mouth and turn, setting the hook himself rather than the angler pulling it away too soon. I'm convinced that this is good advice for bird hunters too, but for a slightly different reason. When it comes to shooting, I try to live by the axiom, "Good things come to those who wait."

Most shots on birds connect at twenty five yards, maybe thirty, tops. If you've patterned your shotgun, you know an Improved Cylinder choke at thirty yards creates a pattern about three feet in diameter. At twenty yards, it's tiny, often just two feet wide. With that condensed shot cloud there is little chance of actually hitting something unless your bead is dead-on. It's why we can flock-shoot and still miss every bird . . . the spaces between birds can be bigger than our shot cloud!

When the birds fly, take a moment to focus, and I don't mean just your eyes, but your head too. Your pattern will open up, evening the odds a bit, and with more space between covey birds, you might not be as tempted to flock shoot . . . as often.

See Better

Still not hitting them? You might be cross dominant. Your "off" eye may be stronger than the one looking down your gun barrel. If you miss a lot and always to one side, you could be one of the ten percent of us (me included) who need to cope with this condition.

Are you one of us? Here's a simple test: Keep both eyes open, extend one arm, index finger pointing up as if it's a rifle sight. Look over your "sight" and put an object across the room on top of it. Close the eye that normally looks down your gun barrel (for right-handed shooters, this will be the right eye). If the object doesn't move from the top of your "sight," you're not cross dominant. If it jumps to one side, welcome to my world.

Depending on your motivation and self-discipline, take your pick of these solutions:

• Learn to shoot using the opposite eye and shoulder.
• Shut your dominant eye while shooting (good luck).
• Wear shooting glasses and put a patch over your dominant eye.

The patch handicaps my dominant eye. So does Buddy.

The patch method eliminates a summer's worth of frustration while learning to shoot again (or in my case, two summers). It also allows shooters to focus (pardon the pun) on the bird, not trying to remember to close your eye while shooting.

The key to success here is careful placement of your patch. Use a one-inch piece of transparent tape. Put it on your shooting glasses' dominant eye lens so that when you mount your gun, the muzzle is obscured by the patch. It's not the perfect solution (hard crossers from your dominant eye side will still be tough), but it beats the alternatives.

Whether you are or aren't cross dominant, try to keep both eyes open. Shotgunning is a pointing skill, not an aiming skill. Unlike rifle shooting, we don't line up the rear sight and the front sight. There is no rear sight on a shotgun because our eye serves that purpose. Ideally, we focus on the bird, not the gun muzzle, the rib, or the beads on the barrel, if there are any.

Why Bother?

Remember your dog's primary motivation. My dogs and I get along best when I hit the birds they produce for me. After all, that's their ultimate payback. Putting the odds in my favor is the least I can do. Now, so can you.

A good shot, rewarded.

5

Training . . . Both of You!

"The cheapest part of dog training is what people are the cheapest with . . . birds."
—Bob Pettit

Chill, Man!

I often joke about it, and so do others, but in my heart of hearts I know it's true. Dogs know when they are going hunting. At our house, it could just be a training run. My dogs don't know the difference but they're just as attentive. Our actions, routines, and body language all provide clues that quickly become cues for them. If you doubt me, just watch your dog carefully after a couple of days of training. It's fun time and he knows it!

At our house, it might be lacing up a pair of boots. The distinctive rattle as I take a whistle lanyard off its hook prefaces a run in the woods behind our house. Unless I'm careful, I'll say something to my wife that includes the word "outside." At that point, it's off to the races.

Like the Star Wars "Force," cues have a light side and a dark side and can be used for good and not-so-good. Timed incorrectly, our unwitting cues can amp up the energy level and create a free-for-all, setting back whatever training accomplishments we'd previously achieved. Used strategically, they can have a positive effect on your training session, even your hunt.

While excited dogs are often a good thing, bad things can happen when the intensity level gets too high. Base instincts take over and rational thinking goes out the window, leading to inattention or disobedience, which causes us to raise our voice or resort to physicality. Like the Cold War arms race, the tension can escalate with no end in sight, turning a training session into mutually assured destruction. All hope of a productive training session or relaxing day afield flies out the window when we, or our dogs, have a meltdown. At times it's just better to go back inside, decompress, and start over later.

Mellowing the vibe is critical, but it's easier said than done and flies in the face of human nature. We expect dogs to "listen to reason," see our point of view, or simply simmer down when we tell them to, often loudly and frequently. But a psyched-up hunting dog is often just beyond the point of reason, so we need to take it down a notch via a calmer, baser level of communication. Using some of the same cues that set things off can also set things right.

Your voice and your actions can dial down your dog's energy level. It requires discipline on your part, but the end result is worth the effort: a calm dog, ready to take direction and less inclined to do something that could lead to embarrassment (for you) or injury (for him).

Try breaking your routine and thus the visual and aural signals that lead to chaos. Rather than grab a leash and put on your coat preceding the usual nighttime walk, reverse the order, and put some time in between the two acts. At our house, the sounds of electronic collars beeping to life mean time for a training run—the highlight of the day for my dogs. Once they have been beeped into a whirling-panting-run mode, I can't get them to hold still to put the darned collars on them!

When dogs frantically jump at a gate ready to explode with anticipation at being let in—or out—turn your back to them rather than barging through and grabbing at them. If the chaos resumes when you reach for the latch, turn and walk away a few steps. If they want to get through the gate, they'll eventually put two and two together. Barking dogs are often met with yelling by their owner, encouraging them to "be quiet" at maximum volume. Where's the logic in that?

Body Language

To a dog, actions speak louder than words. Move slowly, and you literally demonstrate to your dog that things are not as exciting (or distracting) as they seem. I'm lucky in that I often watch myself on TV (someone has to pump up the Nielsen ratings). I learned to be a teacher the same way—with video. It is a cruel but fair instructor, that small screen. It clearly shows me what I have been doing wrong. But you don't need a camera to reflect on your actions and the messages they convey. Just think before you act, adjust your pace, consider the magnitude of your movements, and your dog will get the message. He actually does that now, but it's often to your detriment, and you might not even know what's causing it.

When words are required, a whisper is often better than a growl. It certainly brings down the adrenaline levels, calming the situation. Like people, dogs will

A light touch is all this shorthair needs.

often pay closer atten-tion to you if you make it hard for them to hear what you're saying. Drop the volume level and you might be pleasantly surprised at the results. Be sure to make eye contact with your dog so that you know that he is (at least partially) paying attention.

Even physical praise has degrees. As I write this, I'm scratching my old-est dog's neck following a quiet "Here" command. It's a slow, relaxing touch, light and low-key. He, in turn, is lying down, expecting nothing but the joy of being near me as his reward for a small job well done—all he did was show up. A vigorous, two-hand rib tickle implies something else entirely, infusing the situation with higher energy and more excitement. It might be just the ticket to jet-propel a long retrieve by my two-year-old . . . to get him going or to be used as a well-earned reward.

A dog that forges ahead when walking at heel is often corrected with a vio-lent jerk on the lead. He, in turn, pulls harder. A pup told to "Whoa" is held still by a taut check cord pulling on his neck. Relaxing that tension would actually put him more at ease, making him more willing to follow the original direction.

Manny simply cannot stand still when he first gets on the training table. I used to yank on his collar, yelling "Whoa" at increasingly high volume. Now I speak calmly, slowly, sometimes from a sitting position, stroking his back until he settles—faster than he ever did when I engaged him in a battle of canine (half) wits.

A Matter of Degree

The education bureaucracy has a term: "Learning Readiness." It is the point when a child has the social skills and physiological abilities to acquire and store information. I'm not advocating electronic collars for children, but there is some crossover. Dogs of all ages need to be ready before they can absorb knowl-edge. Daily routines or unusual situations can destroy that readiness if they raise the energy level beyond his ability to process information.

So, now we've got a calm dog and we're putting him through his paces in the yard. He's going out on "Fetch," retrieving bumpers at incrementally longer dis-tances. At some point, we become so proud of him, so happy with our brilliant

Calm, collected, and ready to learn.

training strategies, that we start yelling praise, ruffling his neck, patting, hugging, stroking, and baby talking a long string of "Good boys."

It's no wonder he comes off the rails.

By supercharging praise, we've dragged our dog down to a baser level of thinking (probably acting on instinct). He's gone from learning mode to wolf-ancestry mode. End of training session.

Here's where fighting fire with fire means matching the type of praise to the level of performance and difficulty of the task. I've never potty trained a child, but I have taught hundreds of kids to play musical instruments. I'm thinking the same principles apply: A difficult skill in the early stages of mastery by a young individual probably requires frequent positive feedback. As the individual matures and understands better what is expected and has some measure of skillfulness, praise should become more measured and direct.

Back to training dogs. Coming when called for the first time at obedience class probably merits a lift off the ground, an all-out hug and sloppy kiss. Once your dog is steady to wing and shot, a quiet "Good dog" or light stroke along his back may be enough praise. A hell-bent-for-election, high-energy hunter

freaking out as you load your shotgun may benefit from a little calm talk, possibly a slow walk-at-heel before you unclip his lead.

The same goes for correction techniques. A capital offense by a mature dog probably merits the verbal equivalent of the electric chair, or collar, but only when the dog is caught red-handed doing something forbidden. But, a minor infraction deserves a traffic ticket. I've developed a repertoire of verbal, physi-

This cocker needs little verbal praise on an easy "walk at heel."

Seldom is the nuclear option
really needed.

cal, and electronic corrections that fit
each crime. At the police academy,
they call it a "Continuum of Force,"
a gradual escalation of strength
responding to threat. Strategically
applied, corrections move the learning process forward without upsetting
the emotional apple cart and bringing
the training process to a crashing halt.

A low-volume growl is my go-to
fix for minor offenses. Volume and sharpness increase as needed. Some trainers
add a pinch collar in their correction repertoire. I'm not above a push or shove
(litter mates and parents did it) when appropriate, but I avoid hitting. I like
electric collars, using the "tone" feature for some misbehaviors, and (seldom)
minimal stimulation for major screwups.

Body language can serve a similar purpose. A little acting experience
helps. An angry face speaks volumes to a dog. I'm not above waving my arms
and stomping my feet to make a point. With some dogs withdrawing your
attention by turning away is a powerful correction, depriving a social animal of
social interaction. Again, let the punishment fit the crime, and when in doubt
err on the side of lighter until you've got your correction chops dialed in.

Benjamin Franklin said, "Moderation in all things." Influencing your dog's
behavior with controlled words and actions is a good place to start.

Eliminate Distraction

I continue to learn almost daily, and one thing I've discovered is that successful dog training is about control. Sure, it's control of your dog's actions, but it's
also control of every situation. Delmar Smith's axiom about never giving a dog a
chance to fail has relevance here, too. By eliminating variables in a training situation, you minimize the likelihood of failure. And when it comes to training, I
need all the help I can get!

A dog progresses down the learning path by being introduced to skills and
then mastering those skills in the face of growing distraction. Those distractions
should be introduced and controlled by you, at the right time, in the right place.
Because dogs are linear thinkers, it makes sense to carefully lead them (sometimes literally) from Point A to Point B to Point C, rather than cross your fingers
and hope for the best.

So well trained even two cameramen don't faze him.

Think about it. The concept of "yard training" is a fundamental way to introduce basic training concepts with minimal distractions to young dogs before exposing them to the dog park, downtown, or the hunting field and the chaos that often reigns in those places.

We'll discuss later the required tools to have on-hand prior to training. First, let's talk about what we don't need at initial training sessions. Initially, avoid having other dogs and people around. Being a social animal, your dog will be as interested in other beings as he is in you. Despite your pleadings and their best intent, spectators will invariably do something that's not part of your training strategy. They'll talk, move, bark, praise, cough, sneeze, shuffle feet, and pee (the dogs, not the humans). There will come a time to introduce people and other dogs—as distractions in a long-term training strategy—but early in the development of basic skills is not one of those times.

More subtle, but just as important, are the mental preparations, surroundings, and gear you will use. The day you forgot the check cord will be the day your dog bolts after a frisky whitetail when he's supposed to be on point. Or, the one time you failed to consider wind direction will be the time you release your dog on the upwind side and he crashes, painfully, into the bird launcher.

My electronic collars are always charged, so if or when I need one, it is ready to go.

When training I prefer not to improvise or cut corners. When working with young dogs on the retrieve, I put bumpers along a fence line so my pup is encouraged to run a straight line out and back. If I want him to find a bird or bumper quickly to instill confidence and reliable performance, I make sure it lands where it's visible to him. During dicey retrieving or search challenges, I carry an extra "throw bird" so if a young dog's intensity lags because he can't find the "bird," I quickly toss the second bumper and turn the situation into a win.

"Heel" is a simple obedience command, but early in the learning process I use curbs, fences, and walls to ensure compliance.

Even before a TV shoot, I set the stage, commanding a "Whoa."

Birds complicate matters exponentially. They are probably what inspired the cliché "What can go wrong, will go wrong." Gabbing with your training partner while you reach into the bird box almost guarantees an escaped bird and a chasing dog. Take the time to dizzy a pigeon and today will be the day he walks off or flies away before you can get a check cord on your pup and work him into the scent cone. Plant a bobwhite without marking the spot with flagging tape and odds are you'll forget its location. A controlled find-point-flush session becomes a Chinese fire drill.

Quail waiting in the box for later use are kept out of sight and smell from my dogs, solving one common problem, but what about those "strong flyers" you bought from a local bird raiser that refuse to get airborne, or when your dog scoops a bird up because you forgot to bring your bird launcher? Or my nemesis, pigeons that fly to the nearest tree, where they unknowingly taunt my freaked-out dog, who is baying and pacing underneath? We train in the desert for a reason!

I confess! I overuse my training table. My dogs probably get bored with the warm-up drills they go through on it before their minds are truly challenged in other locations. But setting the stage gets us all in the training mode and helps me maintain control over many of the wild cards we will surely be dealt.

What's the key to a happy training scenario? Know beforehand what you plan to accomplish. Anticipate the gear and situation you need to ensure a successful session. Get rid of extraneous stuff and distractions. Maintain control over as many of the variables as possible.

"Hope for the best and plan for the worst" is another shopworn cliché that has earned a place on every trainer's kennel wall, and for good reason. By carefully orchestrating training situations, you've done both.

Break It Up

Some dog trainers use the term "chaining" to describe the process of one step in the training progression leading to another. That's the good side of the coin. The evil twin is when you mistakenly link one behavior to another and all your great training goes out the window.

Often, mistakes happen out of convenience, or because we never stopped to think the process through. The result is a dog that puts two and two together to make three, even when we want him to come up with four or five.

I'm as guilty as anyone, and here's a prime example: My first two wirehairs were, well, let's just say on their own when it came to the nuances of bird hunting and associated training. I wasn't a very good owner, and they took advantage of my naïveté. Without knowing it, my dogs "chained" many of my commands to verbal praise and that praise into a release.

Here's what I mean: Young dog comes. Once he arrives, he gets an ear scratch and "Good dog." Presto! He's off on another adventure. The problem is, I never released him and didn't want him to run off. This took mere weeks for my dogs to learn—and years for me to figure out that I had trained them that way.

There are many times when you don't want your dog doing what he'd naturally do next in a progression of behaviors. A dog on "Whoa" may have learned (thanks to your inattention) that his next command is always "Go hunt" or "Fetch." He might have figured out that the sound of flapping wings or "boom" leads to "Fetch." But at the edge of a cliff, any of those could be fatal. If your dog has trained himself by default (with your unwitting help), the situation can become a dire one.

He hasn't yet learned to "chain" a point with a flush.

My dogs, even after years of futile attempts, still try to dash off the moment they arrive in response to my "Here" command. Now I count to ten in my head, as much for my own benefit as theirs, before releasing them. Sometimes, I'll next command "Heel" instead of "All right," to help them stay on their toes.

Many dogs I hunt with at preserves have mastered the "drive through retrieve." They fetch with dash and verve, racing past to drop the bird at their handler's feet, heading out to hunt again before they've even made the delivery. That may be well and good in situations where big-tipping clients want to kill a lot of birds, but it can be counterproductive on a deep-woods grouse hunt when birds are few and spooky.

Whatever the inadvertently learned string of behaviors, it pays to break them up, adding some time between them to reinforce their independence from each other. When you ensure that each command is discrete and distinct, each response becomes a full and complete task that stands on its own. It has a start and a finish, rather than simply being a detour en route to somewhere else. You might try inserting a pause, putting some time in the margin between one command and its release, or between one command and another, or change up the usual order of commands.

Try calling your dog to you. When he arrives, touch him for several seconds, maybe hold tight to his collar. Maintain his attention, too—call his name, or use eye contact. Early on, don't provide a food treat the moment he slams into your shin—wait a few seconds. Like a magnet, your attention will keep him there until you give him permission to bolt.

I like to vary the length of time between commands that are frequently chained together. For example, the tail-end of a "Fetch" command doesn't necessarily mean the immediate relinquishing of the bird. My dogs are often asked to hold the bird for a while, standing at my side before the "Give" command is voiced. I've yet to hear a gripe from my dogs about that one, but when I "Whoa" them before unclipping the lead for the first hunt of the day, they are baffled at my cruelty.

A collar touch—or a hold on youngsters—breaks the cycle.

Picking up your own bird keeps a dog on his toes.

A variation on this change-up may be used when steadying a dog on point. If he's associated every point with a flushed bird, every flushed bird with a gun shot, and every gun shot with a retrieve, the temptation to bust the bird is sometimes irresistible. He wants to run through the progression as quickly as possible, but that is not always our goal. Good trainers often do their own retrieving for this very reason, or don't shoot every bird that flushes. They want their dogs to stay put until they are told what to do next. At the minimum, you can slow things down and stretch the interval between shot and "Fetch."

Think about your dog and some of the frustrating things he does. You might be surprised at how many are the result of your unintentional "training." Most can be minimized by adding a long pause between commands.

They Are All Blind

Waterfowl hunters have a term called "blind retrieve," where the dog doesn't actually see the bird drop, yet is trained to streak right to the duck and bring it back. After watching video from the camera I mounted on Buddy, it seems to me that nearly every retrieve is a blind one, at least from the dog's perspective.

Anything taller than your dog can bollix up a retrieve.

It's a matter of geometry. A dog is low to the ground. His line of sight to something else on the ground is invariably obstructed by bushes, rocks, even high spots in the terrain. The obstruction doesn't have to be very tall—a few inches will suffice, and your bumper or dead bird is virtually invisible to the searching dog.

Buddy's field of vision is too low to allow him to see beyond even short cover. When we are hunting in the tall stuff, I'm just glad he has a good nose.

Try it yourself sometime. Lob a bumper into the brush, kneel down, and see what you can—and can't—see.

To counter this I send Buddy in on the downwind side of where I thought a dead bird landed. This allows him to use his nose and invariably leads to a successful retrieve—blind or not.

The Inevitable Setback

Have you ever let your dog out of the truck and while loading your shotgun wondered if he'd lost all his marbles on the drive to your covert? Or, while making progress on a new skill, he suddenly develops amnesia? Just as when you learned to drive, speak Spanish, or hit a baseball, your dog experiences setbacks. He hits plateaus, he backslides, and at the end of the day you're left holding the birdless bag.

Was he taken over by pod people? Not really. If this happens to you, take heart, because sometimes my dogs act like that too.

The good news is that those speed bumps flatten out with time. The bad news is that you can set him back even farther if you harangue and harass him when he's just not getting it. It may be time to step back and take a deep breath.

First, stop and think. Make sure you're communicating clearly and that your dog understands what you want him to do. Take stock of the learning process up to that point. Warm up with the skills he knows that lead up to the one you're drilling into him. Try it again. If he's still looking at you like you're from Mars, stop. Go back a few steps or switch to a different, mastered skill. End on a positive note. Sometimes it's best to leave the more difficult stuff for another day.

Safety in Numbers

How often should you train your dog with others? The saying goes "Many hands make quick work," but dog training is not just about instant productivity. All dogs learn at their own pace, and sometimes a slow, steady progress can be more productive.

Every hunter has a story or two to tell. When talking about hunting spots they're willing to share, or when reading between the lines of a pedigree. Listen and learn because there could be a nugget of useful information on a training technique or a piece of gear you can't live without (okay, several pieces).

Welcome help, even if it's just holding your dog while you mount up.

But there's more. Watching other dogs work will make you think of your own dog. Pitching in, your on-the-ground observations take on added relevance for your own situations. Do you see your own dog in others? Somebody might have a different solution to your problem, or you might discover there's a better brand of beef jerky.

In medical schools the process is watch-do-teach. It may not necessarily count as formal "teaching" when we trade chores like planting birds, but the lessons are there for the taking.

A Little Cushion Ensures Success

Buddy is reliably steady to wing-flush-shot-fall. He'll bring virtually every bird that falls all the way back to me . . . most of the time. Birds are a bit of a challenge because they're odd-shaped and often still alive and kicking, each presenting a unique challenge for the dog. But he's just about there. Mostly. I hope.

To get us across the finish line, I have added a buffer, or cushion, at the end of each retrieve.

Many trainers suggest running away from the dog as he returns with the bird, sparking the chase instinct. I see it as extending the "buffer" between handler and dog indefinitely. My thinking is that the dog is inclined to hold the bird until he thinks you can or want to take it. If he can't get close enough for that transaction, he keeps holding on to the bird. It works in training but eventually you'll have to quit the tactic because field trial and hunt test judges will mark you down a few points after they stop laughing.

I've added my own twist on this strategy, and it's become a helpful transitory step. I'll run away but let Buddy gradually catch up. As he gains ground, I reverse field, quickly close on him, and grab the bird while giving the release command. The cushion has disappeared immediately, surprising Buddy, and he doesn't have time to drop the bird prematurely.

Or, I'll face him, slowly backing up (stretching the cushion) so he is encouraged to continue his approach (much like running away), but with a "soft" stop. I watch him carefully and if I see any hint of premature release, I'll back up faster.

He won't drop the "bird" if he thinks it will fall off the training table.

The real epiphany for me was using the "Whoa" table in a new way. Most of our introductory lessons took place there, so Buddy knows when he's on the table it is all business. Sending him on a retrieve from the table, he knows to return to the table. Now I'm taking advantage of that training in another way.

When he comes back, I'll move a few feet away from the table, where he's forced to stop short of me. He can't put the bird down because he's at the edge of the table and it would fall farther than he's willing to reach to pick it up again, providing yet another "cushion."

Once he's stopped and holding, we're on to a longer hold. This is more a test of my will than Buddy's, and I'll talk about that soon.

Praise Is Not a Release Command

We see it all the time in the field, on TV (even I'm guilty), and in the show ring. A praiseworthy performance merits a ruffled ear, scratch, back stroke, food treat, or "Good boy," and the dog is outta there. The problem is, he shouldn't be—yet.

We get ourselves in deep kimchi when praise becomes a release command. Think about it: dog does well, we praise, he learns to scoot away as if we'd said, "Okay." How does this impact more complex skills that require stops and starts, particularly during the training process?

Take the retrieve, for instance. We first teach a dog to hold the bird. While he holds, we praise. Brought up incorrectly, he might interpret that as "All done," drop the bumper, and go off to play. When the dog is standing a bird, once he's steady and we murmur "Good dog" or stroke the underside of his tail, he may flush the bird if he thinks that early praise is the same as saying, "Okay."

In the simple mind of a dog, praise has a lexicon all its own. It has a time and place; it's a complex vocabulary. But it has no relation to my release word, so I make sure there is never a doubt in my—or the dog's—mind about what is expected of both parties.

This dog knows what is expected of him at this moment, "Hup."

Sweet Release

Clear commands are essential. But what about after a dog is "Here," or is at heel, or has successfully responded to any other command or task you've given him to perform?

Once the bird has flown or your dog has arrived at your side, you really only have three choices: release him to do what he wants, give him another command, or just go about your business and let the dog decide what to do next, essentially allowing him to take charge of the situation.

I prefer to choose one of the first two. As the old saying goes, "The job's not over until the paperwork's done." A dog trainer's "paperwork" is another command or release. Issuing the next command will be addressed elsewhere, but here, let's talk about release.

A dog that knows his place in your pack order is most comfortable being told what to do. Anarchy is not part of the wolf pack demographic—a litter of pups does not rule the bitch. There is a structure, a protocol to virtually everything a dog does. Without order, chaos reigns, and dogs don't like chaos.

A dog that hasn't been told what to do will sometimes go off the rails, and none of the variations are pleasant. He'll decide there is no pack leader and try to become the dominant personality (aggression and fighting being the ultimate expressions), or he'll slink off to seek a more orderly situation. These are just two of the possibilities.

The pack made up of you, your family, and your dogs works best when expectations are clear. When a dog completes a task, it's time for you to issue his next assignment. Give clear direction to your dog on what to do next. The command may be "Go play," or "Do what you want," but it must be given, by you, to him.

Slow and Steady Wins the Race

Dogs are amazing creatures. Given time, they can master virtually any simple skill. It's a matter of conditioning—small, incremental steps ultimately lead to the whole package. I've talked elsewhere about how distance is one of those increments, how eager dogs can maintain self-control in the face of exciting stimuli if you are close enough to influence them.

Another aspect of this incremental teaching involves the speed of those stimuli. I learned this while teaching Manny to be steady to flushing pigeons.

As predators, dogs are hardwired to chase moving objects—after all, dinner is getting away! The faster something moves, the more enticing the temptation to chase it. A bird in my hand that is fast-pitched toward the stratosphere reaches deep into Manny's DNA, getting him fired up and racing after it in a flash.

Speaking of DNA, one trainer I know suggests a dog has at least two mind-sets or "brains." There's the normal canine "brain," or thought process. But with too much simulation, he reverts to his "lizard brain," reacting and relying on instinct, not thought. Once there, it can be a while before he regains his normal senses.

Back to the training session: When Manny watches a pigeon being pulled slowly from my vest, deliberately placed on the ground, and then slowly prodded by a gentle push skyward into a slow-motion "flush," I am rewarded with a steady puppy. In a week, the motion is sped up. A week later, the bird flies all by itself. Eventually, the dog will be cool, calm, and collected, even as birds fly from under his nose when thrown at warp speed.

Take It Down a Notch

I am the master of the setback. Actually, my dogs are. They know exactly when I've become too cocky, over-confident, full of myself. That's when they go south on me.

Plateau, brick wall, resistance . . . whatever word you use, sometimes your forward progress is a baseball meeting a Louisville Slugger. All that masterful teaching is shattered into tiny shards of brilliance littering the pavement like a windshield after a high-speed collision.

Sometimes, I give a command for a skill the dogs are close to mastering, but suddenly they act as if I am speaking another language. A routine retrieve turns into a keep-away game. Walking at heel devolves to a tug-of-war. Maybe you know what I'm talking about. If you don't, you don't own a dog yet.

One thing is clear in these situations: belaboring the point, trying to power through the problem, getting loud and insistent, seldom works. Think again about that employer-employee relationship I talked about earlier. Dogs are less

Leave the field rather than let the situation go farther down the drain.

inclined to do anything for someone who belittles, intimidates, or threatens them. Their instinctive reaction to a screaming, flailing human is fear—accompanied by confusion or flight. In any case, your actions are not instilling confidence in them.

That's when it's time to dial things down a bit.

Step back. Inhale deeply. Try to think like a dog, seeing things from his perspective. If you're lucky, you'll figure out that you are part of the problem. Poor communication is number one on my hit parade of screwups. The problem could be too much distraction, or you might have thought he's mastered a skill when he really hasn't.

Rather than continue teaching hesitancy and doubt, step back on the learning continuum to a point in the skill set where you know he's well versed. Go back into the yard rather than the field and its distractions. Or go quickly to a familiar command where the outcome will be positive.

Get past the obstacle, go have some fun. There's always tomorrow.

The Nose Knows

After decades of doing everything the hard way, I came up with the axiom, "Follow the hunter with the longest nose." That reminder of who's really in charge in the field has served me well over the years.

Which way will this guy go?

Dogs are essentially sniffing machines propelled by furry bodies. Their lives are ruled by their noses, and if we're smart we will let that appendage dazzle us in the field. But there is a dark side to a critter ruled by his schnozzola, and like the Force we must master it, and then employ it for good.

Watch your dog's nose and where it's pointed when you prepare to send him into the field, or after a retrieve, or on the breakaway at a field trial or hunt test. Most dogs adhere to my axiom (so to speak), following *their* nose. They will run along their line of sight. For this reason, don't release him until his nostrils are aimed at your objective.

Watch a great retriever trainer send his dog for a blind retrieve. He'll first get that dog sitting still at his heel. Then, he'll put a hand over and in front of the dog's head to give the dog something to focus on, right down the line toward the destination. Once the dog is sent, he is naturally going to follow the hand-nose-line-bird route unless he encounters a compelling distraction.

Observe a pointing dog field trial handler and you'll see him angle his dog's head slightly away from his bracemate. When the senior judge says, "Let 'em go," the dogs streak away in different directions. Unless it's me and my dog! He will be facing north yet I'll ask him to head south or east. His body may well

He'll probably hold this point better—his body can't easily follow his nose.

be lined up with the field I want him to work, but his head is cocked ninety degrees so off he goes into the other field, but it's not necessarily his fault; it could be that I'm a slow learner.

There are benefits to this knowledge: Got a dog that bolts through your gate? "Heel" him up to it, but facing away or at right angles to the gate. Even more useful, I've found that a young dog will often be steadier in the presence of live birds when he's "pointing" from an oblique angle. Early in his career, I try to bring my dog into a bird's scent cone from the side so that he is assaulted by a sudden cloud of thick scent, surprised into a point. It's a useful training step as you bring birds closer and introduce flushers and fliers.

Watch your dog closely. In training, testing, hunting, even obedience, you'll probably find other ways to use your dog's nose for purposes other than sniffing out wily ringnecks.

For Every Action . . .

You've heard the phrase "Less is more." Does it have relevance to dog training? You decide . . .

Buddy and I were deep into preparation for an upcoming NAVHDA Utility test. It's a tough test, full of anxiety-producing drills. Both the field and water portions require a dog to be rock steady in the midst of distraction shots, walking birds, flying birds, dead birds, shot birds, bobbing decoy, and swinging guns. Not to mention a small gallery of judges, gunners, and handlers adding to the circus-like atmosphere. And, did I mention the steadiness thing?

Wham! It hit me during a less-than-stellar moment when, with my wife's help on the check cord, Buddy lunged every time the bird flew and the gun popped. Here was the revelation: Buddy was reacting to her tensing the check cord, holding on for dear life in anticipation of the bid's flush and his rush. She was telegraphing that tension to him literally and figuratively. He felt both physical and emotional stress and simply couldn't focus on what he knew to be right.

An obedience trainer who'd worked with wolves once told me canines will almost always pull back when you do, for example, on a lead. We use this to our advantage when steadying a dog on point by pushing on his rump. In my case, just the opposite was taking place.

None of this would have sunk in nearly as quickly had I not taken him out to remedy the situation with a brush-up the next day, sans spouse. No wife, no check cord, no tension in the air, and *voila!* A steady dog throughout the sequence.

Bad Birds

Back when I was younger (not much) and more naive (very much) I learned the hard way that a wing-clipped pigeon is sometimes not the best retrieving tool for a young dog.

We were working on steadiness in the face of running birds, and that part we'd finally gotten down pat. But, as the saying goes, "Perfect practice makes perfect," so I concluded that a retrieve should finish the drill.

Katy bar the door! Even a wing-clipped bird can make quite a dust cloud once a dog joins the tumble. A live, unencumbered bird is a different animal than a dead one. I doubt one could call it "fighting back," but pigeons can put up considerable resistance with beak-and-nail and wings akimbo, which was the primary obstacle, it turns out.

For a while, the outcome was in question, but eventually, retrieves were made and culinary kudos handed out to canine participants. But not without some confusion. Later sessions better simulated the "dead bird" scenario, with wings wrapped to avoid head-in-the-mouth and even less stable retrieving grips. We're much happier now.

Distance Learning

At a recent training day, I had an epiphany. I don't know if my partners thought so, but it hit me like a gulp of cold coffee, and I've alluded to it earlier. Here's the full story.

I'd already put Buddy in his crate after two or three good executions of a command. Why tempt fate? Meanwhile, the other trainers wanted to steady their dogs on thrown pigeons. I volunteered to throw. We had a young setter, an older wirehair, and a relatively mature shorthair in the field staring at the same bird, held by yours truly.

I had a revelation while choreographing the three-dog rodeo and believe it has relevance to training of all types. After a couple of less than successful attempts, we set the dogs in a line, most advanced in front, youngest farthest away from me and the bird. This put the greatest temptation nearest to the mature dog, while the young setter was in the next time zone, far from the sound, sight, and smell of a fluttering, flying pigeon.

Young Manny (top) slid into this honor at a distance, so he isn't tempted to steal the point.

It worked, and I've been employing the technique ever since on my own steadiness drills with guns and birds. We're concentrating on steady to wing-shot-fall, and it really makes sense. Day to day, and even over the course of a single training session, I begin in the distance, and then work slowly closer to Buddy. It's likely that your dog has a "zone," too, and as long as you're outside it he won't break when pressured by fluttering wings and loud bangs.

Are there other training scenarios where distance helps a dog cope with new challenges, such as first encounters with other dogs or meeting other people? How about his first exposure to a decoy rig? Or honoring another dog's point? A horse used by field trialers, or the gallery during hunt tests also come to mind.

Just as distance works for some situations, proximity is better for others. Early in their education, many dogs are placed on a lead or check cord so the handler can have immediate control on skill acquisition, correcting, directing, or guiding in the process.

But even when the lead is unclipped, some skills are better mastered by a dog kept close to his master, giving the impression that he's still physically linked. "Whoa," for example, is best taught while you're near enough to grab a collar. Steadiness in the presence of flushing birds is mastered more quickly when the handler is alongside the dog, soothing, praising, possibly putting pressure on his flank as the bird clatters skyward.

A dog that's still got a metaphorical umbilical cord will likely fail less often, quickly mastering each skill.

"Hold," Please

Once a dog is solid on retrieving and is holding well a bird or bumper, it is a matter of extending that hold indefinitely. This is critical in almost every hunt test or field trial situation, and is crucial in the field. Wing-clipped birds are highly motivated to scoot away given the chance, and that chance occurs when a dog puts it down before the handler has his hands on it.

So, how are Manny and I working through this? Well, we are making progress. As I said earlier, it's often more a test of *my* will than Manny's. I have to resist giving the release command too soon while trying to preempt him from dropping a bird. When he beats me and drops the bird anyway, I give it back without repeating the retrieve command. Now he's to the point where, when he drops early, a stink-eye look from me is enough to clue him into picking up the bird again. I move away to encourage the pickup and a completed retrieve.

When Manny is holding well, it's my job to help by minimizing distractions or confusion. Confusion comes in many forms: leaning forward, premature praise, reaching into the pocket I hide treats in, reaching for the bird, or extending a hand, even if it's to praise with a stroke along his backbone.

Instead, I use gestures to encourage holding, and to distract Manny from releasing until he hears that command. I will back up slowly so he never knows when the retrieve is actually completed. I stand up straight, show him empty hands (which means no treats, keep your mouth closed on the bird). I'll wave one hand high to keep his head up (which encourages holding). Meanwhile, the other hand is ready below Manny's mouth for a surprise "drop" command when he least expects it.

I know professional dog trainers have other techniques, from toe pinch to electronic collar "stimulation," but early in a dog's career I'm inclined to avoid the connection of a bird in the mouth to any pain, emotional or physical.

A Place for Everything, Including Learning

Even the greatest of trainers have had a great dog that seemed to lose all his marbles on that first real bird hunt. This often happens because the dog was trained in the same location every time. Keep in mind that dogs are "place learners," associating a particular command with the spot where they learned it. But in the real world, pup has to learn to obey or perform a command no matter where he is. Training him in a number of locations becomes critical so he doesn't come off the rails on the next hunt or field trial. So, when planning your training regimen, don't forget your travelin' shoes.

Drill, drill, drill . . . in your house and yard. Once your pup knows a command, take it on the road. Go to town, friends' houses, different fields, places with new distractions. Even at home, you can move from front to back yard, inside to outside, or even across the street. All of these help the dog to focus on you and your command, ignoring the attractive diversions a new place may offer.

Pro trainers will tell you a dog isn't trained until he performs a command flawlessly in seven different places. Unless, of course, it's me and my dog Buddy. Then it will probably be *seventeen* places.

Timing Is Everything

If you have a good relationship with your pup, he looks to you for direction, literally. The trick is to give him direction *when he's ready to take it*. I call it the

This pup is looking at me (out of frame)—time to give a command.

"Golden Moment," and it makes training much more effective. You're helping your dog succeed by arranging all the variables in his favor, including his ability to process your command.

Watch your pup. He'll cock an ear your way, glance at you, sometimes even stop and look. If needed, get his attention by calling his name. Another opportune moment is when he's just about done with that bathroom stop. All are perfect opportunities to direct him.

The US Army says you have a little more than a second to give a command before something smellier or more fun will grab his attention. Pay close attention to your dog's actions, pauses, gestures, and pace in the field. You'll soon be able to read him like a book.

When you do your part right and he executes his command, you've also got a second to praise him. A second after that his gears have shifted and he won't make the connection to his good deed. (Remember he thinks linearly.)

The Golden Moment is also critical when it comes to correcting your pup. Catch him before he's committed physically and mentally to his infraction, and you can usually nip bad behavior in the bud. Wait a little too long and he's not going to listen, let alone obey, so save your breath. He won't make the connection between deed and punishment.

Timing is everything, even when dog training. You just don't have very much!

Two-Edged Sword

Whether or not you can teach an old dog new tricks, I'll save for another day. But can an old dog teach a new dog tricks? You bet!

Old-timers used to say that's how a young bird dog learned . . . he followed a mature dog in the field. I'm not convinced it's the only way, except possibly for hound dogs, nor even the best way. It has a place in training, but it's a two-edged sword.

Master and apprentice share the field . . . sometimes, it works.

With my old dog Yankee, I'd agree. His breeding was, well, let's just say he'll never be listed in the Who's Who of hunting dogs. If there had been a PE major at obedience school, he'd have been one.

But Manny has learned a lot from his uncle Buddy (including some things I wish he hadn't). So I have to be strategic about which commands I use and their timing. I try to limit my "co-teaching" to skills I'm confident Manny has mastered. In those cases, having Buddy's help has jump-started Manny's development.

Staked out, Manny learns by watching when Buddy demonstrates his skills. In the field when I call Buddy, Manny will follow, learning the same command by rote. The converse is also true, so use this trick with caution. When Buddy disobeys and Manny sees it, all my hard work goes out the window.

In the yard or on the table, a mature dog can be almost as good as a check cord, providing a good example by standing steady to a flushing bird. And some dogs, sometimes, are proprietary about retrieves to the point where they'll race for one when another dog might get it instead, even if that dog is on a check cord or staked out. If your pup needs motivation, that can be a good thing.

There is another downside to the old dog–young dog theory: A pup that learns to follow, merely imitating his mentor, is never thinking for himself. A certain amount of boldness is needed in a hunting dog, and followers seldom develop the level of confidence that comes from independent work. When one dog sees another dog not following directions you get confusion. He might even take it as encouragement to break the rules. Or worse, one dog does something right but the other blows it. You praise the good dog, and then the offender comes looking for his treat!

A Pickup Line That Works

Both my dogs are constantly testing me. Pup, sure, but even an adult dog can lose it once in a while, and you've got to intervene. Whether the transgression involves disobedience, aggression, or just some annoying behavior that's getting on your nerves, sometimes you've got to take things into your own hands, literally.

We can use the electronic collar, check cord, or lead, we can scream and yell . . . one at a time or all at once, but they all work on occasion. However, I've discovered another way to break the bad-behavior cycle.

Simply pick the dog up.

Yep, getting all four of his feet off the ground, moving your dog a few feet and putting him down facing a new direction can be the equivalent of hitting the reset button. It's a new day in pup's mind. Maybe it's a bit disorienting, but that's the point. He can't easily continue doing what he was doing when his feet aren't firmly on the ground, and wasn't that the idea?

Once he's "grounded" again, you can continue with training, or just enjoy a little quiet time before continuing his training regimen.

It was a lot easier when Buddy weighed twenty pounds, but a sore back is sure better than having to wade into a dog fight or watching the beginning of a bad habit you'll have to break later.

Toys for Training

The cliché is apt: Dog training is not play. It is often serious business, especially if you're a big-money field trialer. But toys can help your dog grow up when the real thing simply isn't available.

Teaching steadiness? Live birds are best, but when you can't use pigeons or game birds, try one of those wind-up balsawood airplanes. At two bucks apiece,

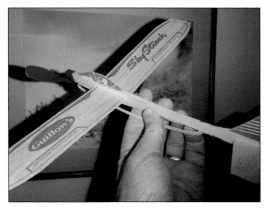

they're a bargain.

Whether you're introducing a pup to gunfire, live in suburbia, or simply feel funny pulling out a real gun, try a cap pistol. It's not as loud or as realistic looking as a shotgun, but it's better than saying, "Bang!"

It's a bird! It's a plane! It's better than nothing.

Don't have practice birds? Or maybe your pup isn't quite ready for them? Paper plates are pretty good imitations. Flying like a Frisbee, up, across, away, and even toward a dog, they imitate a bird well enough, and the price is right.

As the Marvin Gaye song suggests, "Ain't nothing like the real thing, baby." But the next time you're trying to train and you don't have proper gear, try looking into a kid's toy box for inspiration.

Bite the Financial Bullet

The price of a line-bred hunting pup can be substantial, but it will be the least of your financial concerns. It's the other stuff that will hit you in the pocketbook—and quite often. Take my word for it, the following list of gear will make bringing up your own pup a lot easier. Here is my short list of labor-saving, headache-avoiding, puppy-training gear:

A training table saves your back, makes pup a little less confident and more likely to pay attention. You can get plans to build your own table at www.navhda.org.

A tie-out stake teaches pup to yield to the collar, which comes in handy when teaching "Whoa" and "Heel." It's also a safe place to put pup when training his runnin' buddy, or when you've got your hands full elsewhere.

My training table: portable and sturdy.

A check cord ensures that every command you give will be instantly and completely obeyed.

A vest or game bag keeps everything handy while your hands remain free to handle a leash, bird, collar, or check cord.

Save your voice for campfire conversation. Teach pup to respond to your whistle. A whistle won't panic birds like another human's voice, either.

And get some pigeons. Veteran trainer George Hickox was right: no birds, no bird dog.

Depersonalize the Corrections

I like to maintain a positive relationship with my wife, friends, coworkers, *and* especially my dogs. Like the rest of them, my hunting companions don't appreciate "constructive criticism" from me. So, I try to let them think it's coming from somewhere else.

Sure, there are times when the Master has to assert himself over the dog. You simply want him to do—or not do—certain things at certain times. Why not let your training tools take the blame?

The leash keeps Buddy at heel, not my constant haranguing. A check cord becomes the bad guy when Buddy doesn't "Whoa." With both, avoid eye contact as you yank for an extra dose of depersonalization.

When a dog is distracted, the tone feature on the electric collar breaks his train of thought and suddenly I'm not the party pooper. And in rare cases, the collar's

The collar becomes the bad guy.

stimulation comes from out of nowhere, not from me! I even try to hide my hand while holding the collar transmitter.

With this strategy, at the end of the day we're still friends, *and* plenty of learning has taken place. And that is what counts.

Are You a Greedy Owner?

We all have an ego, and like our dog, we need to feed it once in a while. But Buddy has shown me that *too much* of a good thing is bad. Don't become greedy during training, whether it's to reinforce a new skill, show off for friends, or just strive for excellence. There are times when we want just one more repetition from a dog that's already worked overtime, but the results can often be less than pleasing.

After more than a couple of points, Buddy gets bored and loses intensity. The tail drops, and it's obvious that he's phoning it in. He might even start blinking birds. On a long day at a game preserve, that last point can be pretty sad. Or, when the ducks have been coming in droves to your decoys, the limit-capping retrieve may lack a little luster.

Without birds—obedience training, for example—excess can be an even bigger risk. Food treats or your praise pale in comparison to pheasant scent, so your dog may shut down even faster. Step back, assess the day's work, and know when to quit. Remember, there is always tomorrow!

The result of "just one more retrieve."

If you train hard on weekends and not much in between, lackluster performance can be a big issue. But even when training daily, I'm happy with two good performances of any command. The key is to minimize the bad versions with careful preparation and stage managing.

Put it this way: You wouldn't watch a TV show six times in one sitting, not even mine! Why put your dog through the same torture?

Burnout Is a Reality

I'll bet you never did your best work for a cranky, grouchy boss. That's how your dog might feel if your response during training is all negative. At least employers give us money to do jobs we don't like. Dogs can't open a bank account, so that strategy won't work. Instead, the paycheck has to be more subtle.

I don't mean jumping-up-and-down, tail-wagging fun all the time. I mean satisfaction, affection, and appreciation, your dog knowing that his good work is recognized. And remember, in time your dog will mature, grow stronger, and perform to such a high level that he will be asking for more out of you!

For a recent field trial Buddy and I had been training—hard—for quite a while. I was stressed, and he was too. The pressure was on, and I wasn't showing my confidence in him—in fact, just the opposite. And his work was, let's face it, less than stellar. You'd think we'd just met, rather than having worked together for the past five months.

I arrived a day before the trial to explore the grounds and, by sheer luck, became grounded myself. Like a pheasant flushing at my feet it hit me: No dog will do his best work for a grumpy owner . . . it's just not fun! And when our negative actions affect the balance of correction and praise, a dog can shut down.

So, we warmed up with lots of praise and an upbeat attitude. It was more fun than work, full of positive reinforcement and plenty of play time. We spent extra time on the things Buddy does well. When he did well, he knew it. We both got psyched, and the next day, he posted the highest score possible.

Envy May Be a Sin . . .

. . . but it's also a great training tool. If Buddy thinks someone else is having all the fun, he gets jealous. And that's when the training starts. Even our little Corgi stimulates the competitive instinct in Buddy. I use that instinct in training for a number of important skills.

The envy strategy helps teach any skill where you can reward one dog while your trainee has to watch from the sidelines. Retrieving is a good example.

Staked out and watching, most dogs are eager to get into the game. They simply cannot stand seeing other dogs carrying all the birds. When it's time to swap trainees, that first fetch drill is often a slam dunk.

Nearly any task you assign your dog will go more smoothly if he's forced to watch another dog (or human) execute it first. Pack-oriented animals want to work with their leader (you), be around you, smell your skin, curry your favor, maybe become the object of your praise, or earn a treat. We may as well use that desire to teach something.

I would caution you to use treats carefully and avoid any head-to-head competitive situations. You are always number one, but dogs will fight for second position in the pack, especially in a high-energy situation involving food, birds, or other stimuli.

Next time you're getting nowhere in your training, think of how jealous your dog would be if I were giving *you* all the treats.

Hold On!

"Good things come to those who wait." "Timing is everything." They're not just old sayings. Buddy has taught me they are sound training strategies.

I know Buddy often looks confused during training; it's operator error, most times. But if your dog appears to have trouble getting it, maybe he's not ready yet. All dogs mature at different rates. Before a pup can learn a new skill, he must be ready physically, mentally, and emotionally.

Periodically sound out your pup—see if his reaction to your command says, "Huh?" It may be a good time to work on something else. Come back to it later, when that mental switch has been flipped inside the pup. I've gotten more attuned to Buddy's readiness to learn, and often will put off training for a week or two, or five, until he's got his intellectual, physical, or emotional ducks in a row.

Most of us only test or field trial a couple of times each year and hunting season is usually months away, so there's seldom any rush. Often, the most important command you can give yourself is "Whoa" while *you* wait for your pup to grow up enough to handle the skill he'll eventually master.

He's not ready for this stage
of the forced retrieve;
I'll back off.

Keep it Simple, Part Two

Dogs have taught me a lot about hunting, training, and life, the most important being, "Save your breath and thus your sanity." I mentioned earlier that some experts believe a dog can learn 200 words. But my dogs prefer that I tighten up my vocabulary.

For example, who needs "Stay" when you've already told a dog to "Whoa," "Down," "Kennel," or "Sit"? When training, make the command a complete act that concludes only when he is told to do something else. It may take a little more initial training time but the thrift in your lifelong dialogue will be worth the investment.

If he's already got the bird in his mouth, why issue a separate command to keep it there, like "Hold"? Extraneous words squander valuable training capital that could be put to better use. When he's just learning you'll need to repeat the command, use some sweet talk, encouraging words, and maybe a food treat or three. But as he masters a skill, he's plenty smart enough to execute the base command without extra reminders.

A dog will still need to know when he's not doing it right, or when he's done with the job. No matter how good a trainer you are, you will need an all-purpose corrective word—I like "Aagh!" when he doesn't get it right. It's a lot like his mother's correction growl, so he already knows what it means. And commands ultimately need a release. Mine is "All right." It rhymes with no other command word, which is critical. Until you give it, your dog should *keep* doing what you've already asked him—*trained* him—to do.

He's already "Kenneled." Why add "Stay"?

Watch that your praise word is unrelated to and not to be construed as the release. If "Good dog" becomes your default release, think of the chaos to follow a staunch point on a big covey that's rewarded with "Good dog."

Don't Break It

If it never broke, you wouldn't have to fix it. That's what Buddy—and a few dozen professional trainers—have taught me. In other words, it's easier to prevent bad habits from forming *from the day you bring pup home,* than to correct them once they're a problem—chasing birds versus being steady to wing, for example, or rushing a gate. Teaching the right way before a dog learns the wrong way saves a lot of aggravation on both sides and gives you time to reinforce obedience with praise instead of constantly screaming at a dog to stop something he's learned (and you've allowed him) to enjoy.

A check cord or lead can be your best friend when it comes to teaching good habits from the beginning. Get one and use it. Start off on the right foot—in your pup's case, both right feet. You and your dog will be better off for it.

Old Dog, New Tricks, Part Two

Besides being a faithful companion and pretty good bird dog, my old dog Yankee found a place in Buddy's training when he was a pup. Buddy saw Yankee performing, getting praise and treats, and the envy started to percolate. Soon that jealousy had its effect. Buddy was eager to get off his chain and onto the training table because he saw the end result—a good time.

But Yankee also served as a useful distraction when Buddy needed fine-tuning. Virtually every skill is mastered by practice with increasing amounts of distraction. People, traffic, and new surroundings all work, but another dog best serves the purpose.

If you want to teach your dog to back or honor another dog's point, you've got all the ingredients right in the back yard. Simple obedience skills are more difficult to ingrain when another dog is in the picture. "Whoa" is much tougher when a pack mate waltzes by on a leash or, worse, is allowed to join in on the retrieving.

Yankee and Buddy taught me that an older dog has his role in training. But be judicious about it—too much following and imitation make a pup lazy. If you want a bold, confident, disciplined hunting partner, at some point you need to cut the (check) cord and let him learn on his own.

No Freebies

An old trainer once told me to never give away a bowl of dog food. I follow that advice religiously because it helps my dogs be better hunters and citizens. And not just with treats.

How? They earn every speck of praise, edible or verbal. They know I expect them to be on their best behavior all the time. I'm constantly providing positive

They earn it with a "Whoa."

feedback when they deserve it. But, an unearned treat or verbal reward does no one any good. It lowers the bar and diminishes any progress you've made.

It starts with dinner time. Lucky for the neighbors, my wirehairs don't have to sing for their supper. But they do "Whoa" for it. Treats, from dog biscuits to water, are doled out for coming when called or for doing a job well. Even verbal or physical praise is earned—phony "Good boys" only mislead a hunting dog from the real work at hand, and serve to diminish the value of his work.

Use praise and treats strategically. You'll get better performance as a result.

Bits and Pieces

"One step at a time" is more than just a rehabber's mantra. My dogs' training is broken into a series of small skills, each one leading to the next. We don't move ahead until the preceding skill is mastered.

For example, "Whoa" begins with comprehension and mastery of the basic command, and then further mastery through a variety of distractions, to rock steadiness anywhere, anytime. It's easy on the training table. Somewhere else, maybe not. Add another dog and you might have to go back to basics.

Add the sight or smell of bird, and more conditioning is required. Taking the lead off or adding hand signals are more steps to be re-introduced at each level.

Sometimes it's back to square one in the yard, while at other times a step or two back is all it takes. If a dog has been away from a particular skill for a while, my first go-round with him starts on the training table to ensure perfect execution.

Dogs learn gradually, in pieces. Once I divide the skill into workable pieces, we're both going to be much happier.

6

Hunting Better

"One does not hunt in order to kill; on the contrary, one kills in order to have hunted."
—José Ortega y Gasset, from *Meditations on Hunting*

HUNTING IS WHERE the rubber meets the road. We all know the basics: find a good spot, work the wind correctly, shoot straight, and birds end up in the bag. If only that were the case!

There is plenty of room for improvement, and sometimes there are better ways to do some of the things we take for granted in the field. Sure, you can become a good hunter with some basic knowledge and skills. But our dogs can help, usually immensely. Why not learn from our mistakes, benefit from those lessons, and become better hunters, faster?

Your dog will thank you.

Line of Sight

If your goal is to have a steady dog that holds a point even while a bird rattles into the sky, put yourself in his place. Dogs are curious creatures, descended from predators, the top of the food chain. Unlike cats, curiosity probably won't kill your dog, but it could cause him to break on a flushing bird if he feels like he's being squeezed out of the action. There's good reason to be strategic about approaching a pointed bird; obscuring your dog's view of the action could encourage him to move so he can watch the proceedings when you want him to stand still.

He'll stay steady because he can see where the bird will flush.

This was driven home to me in a recent training situation. I'd set up the bird in a launcher so it was hidden by tall sage. I brought Manny in crosswind, and he stopped at the first whiff of pigeon, front leg lifted in anticipation of the joy to come. Unfortunately, to keep him steady I got between him and the bird, very close to him, so I could hold up my hand and shout "Whoa" if necessary.

I was ecstatic at his intensity. I walked in on the bird, turned to the dog, and hit the red button on the launcher. Thanks to me Manny couldn't see the bird rise, and so he jumped left as if on springs, back on point when he landed. From his new vantage point, he could see the arc of the flying bird. There was no intent on his part to break point or chase the bird. He simply needed a vector to follow so when the time came to retrieve he'd know where to go.

And there's the lesson. By marching straight in on a bird, we are effectively blocking our dog's line of sight. Holding a point with adrenaline flowing and guns blazing is hard enough. It's understandable that any smart dog would want to know where the flying bird is headed—after all, if things go well, you'll be asking him to "Fetch it up."

Get High

I've hunted birds with my dogs in both Dakotas, Kansas, and Nebraska. In each state, someone claims it is so flat you can watch your dog run away for three days. Stand on a tuna can they say, and you can watch him run away for a week.

I'd be the last to suggest you get high while hunting, figuratively speaking, that is. But literally raising your altitude a foot or two may just result in an extra bird in your vest. If you can see your dog more often you'll have a few extra seconds to get yourself ready for a safe, straight shot.

Brush, rocks, and variables in terrain often obscure your pointing dog's view of you. As bushes get taller and gullies deeper, they also block your view of him. All the waving tails and eager dog behaviors in the world won't help if your dog is invisible to you, hidden by brambles or boulders. Even on a good day, my dogs blend into the vegetation and are virtually invisible, so when I can't find my dogs, I climb. Not a lot, but enough to use the topography in my favor.

It doesn't matter which of you changes elevation as long as you can see each other.

If your dog is trailing a ringneck in a creek bed, take up a position on the lip of the drop-off. When he's snuffling quail along the bottom of a draw, side-step a few feet up the slope. I've scrambled up railroad grades, sauntered along abandoned dirt roads, and once found my dog on point while squinting down at him from a footbridge.

In rice country, the dikes may not be tall, but they are tall enough once the crop is harvested. Irrigation canal levees also make convenient elevators when your dog is muddling around in the head-high crops alongside them. And if you're "conserving energy" (i.e., being lazy) work your way into the bottom of the draw while your dog works the slopes.

No topography to improve your dog's visibility? Find a convenient stump, rock, or log. Just remember to open or unload your gun in case your elevation is suddenly altered in an unexpected, gravity-induced downward dismount.

And when all else fails, imitate the springer spaniel. A careful, gunless jump gains you a foot or two of visibility, even if you're one of those "White Men Can't Jump" types. Otherwise, carry a tuna can with you.

Finding Fido

It's no wonder so many dogs in the West are named "Sage." The shrub is a mottled gray-brown color, especially during the bird-hunting season, and when motionless on point the dogs resemble the native plant to such a degree that it can be difficult to tell Fido from flora.

This is not a new problem. Bird hunters have crafted and connived ways to track their dogs for centuries. In recent decades, everything from brightly colored vests to dog-mounted flagpoles had been offered. Some survived in trial-by-fire field testing, while others have been relegated to the scrap heap of history.

These days, there are a cornucopia of choices, some low-tech, others as sophisticated as satellites. I've used them all (except the flag, which is just silly). Each has its proponents, advantages, and disadvantages. You might find that an array of choices is best for situational or practical reasons. Here are some you might consider:

You can make things easier by selecting a pup that has a white tail. A safer bet is a bright, bold orange collar. Field trialers often use an extra-wide one, with the "top" dog in the brace wearing blaze orange and the "bottom" dog getting fluorescent chartreuse or yellow. But even a plain old collar in blaze orange pops in the field. Many modern electronic training collars feature a beeper housing that is also brightly colored.

Even in the boonies, he's visible with his orange bandana.

I like a little more visibility on my dogs, so I'll sometimes add a blaze orange bandanna tied around their necks. It's another square foot of safety. They add a bit of dash too. But they don't offer as much coverage as a full-body cape or vest. I'm not criticizing the vest or cape, but their advantages are often outweighed by the body heat they retain or their propensity to rub a dog raw at the inevitable contact points.

On the right day, even a cloud of dust can reveal your dog's location. In my case, a cloud of wildly flushing birds often reveals my young dog's route. Got two dogs? Watch your close-by dog. He will often hear your far-off dog when you can't, pausing occasionally to cock an ear or gaze in his direction.

In this era of high-tech phones, it shouldn't be surprising that GPS can ensure your dog's "visibility." While he's streaking across that field or pottering around a thicket in search of quail, today's GPS collars can pinpoint his latitude and longitude, distance from you, even tell if he's on point. And if he won't come when you blow your whistle, some collars enhance his hearing with a low-voltage reminder. Some of the snazziest collars come with flashing lights (call me when you figure them out), or you can buy the dime store version and duct-tape it to his collar.

It is often said that a blind person's remaining senses become heightened. In a way, it's also true when searching for your out-of-sight dog. Listen carefully and you can hear your dog panting from quite a distance. Jingling collar tags give them away too. A bona fide bell offers a pleasant tinkle or an industrial "bong," depending on its size. There is a downside to this: A dog that is locked on point would need to be very well-trained to jiggle his collar bell at the same time, which means the bell will be silent just when you need it most. At other times (such as when you forget to charge the electronic collar's batteries), simply being stealthy will open the world to such a degree that purely organic sounds emanating from your dog will be enough to reveal his location.

Many electronic collars feature a beeper, hawk scream, or other audible signal to help you monitor his progress and signal when he's locked on point. Some hunters find these artificial sounds annoying, but there are some environments where you'd never find your dog otherwise.

Hearing your dog isn't officially being able to see him; it's just another way to keep track of him. Or, you can buy yourself an orange dog.

"Sit!" And I Mean You!

So, you made it to the top of that chukar hill. Or battled your way through that dog-hair thicket in search of grouse, but now it's time for a breather. You sip some water, swap stories with your buddy, maybe nibble a snack.

Your dog paces back and forth, circles you both, slaloms between your legs, and simply won't sit still. He looks, beseechingly, at his hero (you) for direction, a command, something that gives him purpose for the next few minutes. But you're fully invested in an important joke involving a duck, a rabbi, and a waitress.

Eventually your dog wanders off unnoticed, and when you're dropping shells into your shotgun he's nowhere to be found. When you eventually do find him, he's worn out because he didn't rest when you did.

He will take a break if you will.

The solution is simple. "Sitting still" starts with sitting. And I'm thinking that maybe a dog isn't convinced you're resting unless you're sitting (or even lying down, but that may be going too far). That's what he does, his littermates did, his pack does. It's body language in its simplest form. Doggy see, doggy do. Or doesn't, if you're not sitting.

To make the most of your upland breaks, find a tree to lean on, or at least a dry spot where you can plop yourself down for a few minutes. Your dog will follow suit. It might take a leash to keep him there, but you did bring one, right? Offer him water, maybe a treat too. Pick a shady spot if it's warm, a wind-sheltered nook if it's cold. When he stops panting, he's rested and cooled off, ready for the next covert. And, you know exactly where he is.

Bird-Hunting Tips and Strategies

Just Add Water

Upland game birds need water. Not much, and not necessarily from the usual suspects, but they need moisture almost every day. Unfortunately, they don't usually cooperate as well as they did one day in chukar country when an acquaintance filled his gas tank with fuel and my buddy and I with hope. He predicted birds on a certain creek at a certain time. And he was right, but that was a hot day in a droughty season where water was scarce but plentiful in predictable locations. For all I know, he'd been there the day before and caught them by chance, but I'm still grateful.

One way to shoot more birds is to find their water source, and then put yourself between the two. But if it were easy, there'd be fewer birds in the field and more bragging hunters in the local tavern. Most times, we wander creek bed to draw, swale to spring, searching for elusive game birds that (we think) crave the life-giving fluid. So, why aren't they here?

The fact of the matter is that game birds don't have watches. Weather, time of year, and, for all I know, the alignment of the planets influence a bird's schedule and water needs. Early in the season, they are most likely to head for open water: creeks, streams, or a pond. They will travel some to get it too. Biologists tell us up to a mile, maybe more in a crisis.

To make things worse, all water isn't marked on a map. Springs, seeps, roadside ditches, and irrigation canals all proffer enough moisture to sustain life in a game bird. Watch for green spots in an arid landscape, ask locals, and keep an open mind. I've found birds at cattle tanks and dripping windmill troughs.

Birds will visit a water source once, sometimes twice a day if it's really hot or their diet is comprised of dry materials such as grains. But when, oh when, is the eternal mystery. Midmorning and late afternoon are safe but relative guesses.

After a rain a covey won't have to walk to a traditional water source.

If the wind is right or your route allows it, hunt toward or away from water and you might get lucky. Or plan a route that includes water sources several times during the day.

Or simply trust it to pure dumb luck, as I do. Here's the ringer: Even when blazing sun bakes the hills and desiccates everything in sight, birds don't necessarily need open water. Morning dew will often suffice, as will succulent forbs and grasses. The point being, don't put all your eggs in the hydration basket when you shuck those shells into your Wingmaster.

All bets are off once fall rains arrive.

Precipitation resets the balance, putting moisture in places you might not think to look. After a hard rain, dry desert plants blossom in a series of tiny oases. Every depression in the lava rock holds a cup or two of water. That's plenty for a covey that wants to avoid risking life and wing tromping all the way down the hill to the trilling stream that meant life itself in August. Snow can do the same thing as it melts, or in a pinch, can be eaten. Insect eaters get their share of moisture from their crunchy-on-the-outside, chewy-on-the-inside meals.

Lesson: once fall weather settles in, go farther from the usual water sources to get closer to the birds.

What, No Dog?

Bird hunting is tough in any arena but is much tougher without a dog. If you're between dogs—or for some unfathomable reason choose not to own one, you'll find more birds by thinking like a fisherman and trolling for them.

Game birds would often rather sit tight than fly if they think you'll pass by without noticing them. They are expert hunkerers, skillful skulkers. Given the choices (run, fly, or freeze), holding still is a pretty good option. No avian predators, no fangs or claws can wreak havoc when you're hiding under a buffalo berry bush.

Here's my theory: When you saunter past a sitting bird at a steady pace, the birds think you have no intention of stopping, let alone looking for them. In their minds you're just another predator en route to another location—not a hungry fox or coyote looking intently for a meal.

To put more birds into the air, move slowly and erratically, as you would while blind trolling in your boat. Trollers vary their speed with frequent direction changes. Make your bird-hunting approach a zigzag route too. Stop every few yards but be ready for a flush. Sitting birds may think you've found them and will take their usual evasive action—instant flight.

These tactics make sense for fishermen, but you'll see their value in the uplands as you put more birds in the bag.

Shhhh!

The basic goal in bird-dog training is shooting birds over your dog's point. The moment of truth is one of the most exciting and exhilarating of all, but if you sound like the circus coming to town, you'll scare away every bird in the county. Game birds may not be as spooky as whitetails (although ruffed grouse, snipe, and sharptailed grouse are pretty close), they are still very cognizant of predators and the sounds they make. So, stuff a sock in it.

I've crept to within inches of sitting birds by treading more carefully and taking the jinglejangles off the dog's collar. Even though I own a dozen electronic collars most times I'll go in unplugged. I try to ghost my way through brush, not bulldoze into it. Commands are via hand signals, not voice or whistle. My footfalls mimic those of an elk hunter, not a linebacker.

I like Monday-morning quarterbacking yesterday's game as much as the next guy, but when my mouth is shut, my eyes seem to open wider. I enjoy more of the dog work, catch on quicker to his birdiness, savor the scenery, and shoot more birds.

Watch That Dog

Like most poker players, most bird dogs have "tells." Buddy's actions shout, "Bird in here!" long before he points. His tail wags faster, or his nose rises. His head might drop, or that ground-covering gallop will become a prance.

But none of it matters if I'm not paying attention. I might be gabbing with my partner, admiring the view, or just lollygagging. But the fact is, if I don't see my dog's early indicators, I'll be out of position or totally surprised when the bird gets up. The result is a rushed or long-distance shot, an out-of-range flush, and a thoroughly disgusted dog.

Do you know your dog's indicators? Labrador tails often helicopter in circles. Springers' are like miniature windshield wipers—back and forth. My young dog Manny's nose drops groundward, Buddy's looks like he has been hooked like a fish, that tantalizing smell pulling him, nostrils first, toward the bird.

A young Manny would indicate birdiness by dropping his nose toward the ground.

Many pointers tighten up their quartering pattern as the scent cone narrows. Some dogs "cat dance" the last few steps, walking on egg shells before settling into a point. If you're busy gabbing on your cell phone, you might hear the covey roar over the horizon because you didn't see your dog sliding, skulking, or sneaking into a point.

Keep an eye on your dog. It could mean the difference between a bird in the hand and two streaking away in the distance.

Keep Him Cool

Even on his best day, Buddy's a so-so retriever, but we've come to an understanding. On certain days, he and most dogs would rather share a kennel with a poodle than fetch. It's not disobedience, funny smells, or early-onset Alzheimer's. In most cases it's the heat. Some upland bird-hunting seasons open in early fall, when daytime temperatures can still be in the eighties. Add a little debilitating humidity and you have the perfect recipe for a lousy day afield.

Dogs cool themselves by panting. They can't sweat, so it's all about internal air-conditioning, which brings on the heavy breathing. Plug that system with a hot, dry, feathered obstruction and it shuts down.

You can yell, scream, coax, and threaten, demanding that your dog perform, but you'll be wasting your time. The self-preservation instinct trumps any training. Cut your dogs some slack when the temperature and humidity become the greater obstacles. Hunt early or late in the day, cut the sessions short, and when the tongues start dragging (yours and theirs), call it a day.

If you let things go too far, take immediate action. An overheated dog is a serious and potentially deadly problem.

Luckily, even a young dog will clue you in most times. When he heats up, pay attention. If he seems to have lost interest in hunting and seeks out shade every few steps, leash him up. If he's digging holes to lay in, he's hot. If he doesn't stop panting even at rest, he's at risk.

If your dog is overheating, you'll need to act fast. Get him to shade. Soak him down with your own water if you need to. Wet his head, belly, armpits, and

Overheating makes for strange bedfellows, but a dog's gotta keep cool.

chest. If you have rubbing alcohol in your first aid kit, apply it to the same spots. A cattle trough, pond, stream, or hose are lifesavers—immerse your dog up to his withers if possible.

Keep one eye on the birds and one on your hunting companion. When it comes to your dog, being cool means more than owning the right basketball shoe—it means staying alive.

Slow Down

Running hell-bent for election certainly helps cover more hunting territory. But my old dog Yankee taught me that most times, it pays to slow down. When we do we usually find more birds and enjoy better dog work.

Energetic, enthusiastic dogs can blow right past sitting birds. They could be exhaling when they pass through the scent cone, or a brief wind shift may have pushed the scent trail the other way. Warmer temperatures or thick cover minimize the spread of bird scent and could impact a speeding dog's ability to detect it.

Sometimes, we're the guilty party, going too fast and trying to cover 100 acres of CRP field all at once. A dog will start exploring that yummy hint of scent, and his owner will urge him on. If pressured to move quickly, dogs won't circle the area to get a new vector on scent.

You can help by dialing things down a bit. Cut your own pace. After all, you have all day and it's not a track meet. Most dogs will mimic their owners' speed. Help your dog seek all the birdy spots by moving in a smaller version of his back-and-forth search pattern. If he shows interest, stand still and let him work the area thoroughly. If it looks like he's going too fast and missing birdy spots, go back over those areas—twice if necessary.

Remember, you're not after a gold medal. When the gun goes off, it's the successful conclusion to the hunt, not the start of a race.

A Dog's Kit Bag

Parents will remember when their kids were young and they had to drag a bag full of stuff everywhere they went. Bottles, diapers, blankets . . . the list was only limited by the size of the bag. Wouldn't you do the same for your dog too? A dog's kit bag will certainly be smaller, but it will be just as helpful—to both of you.

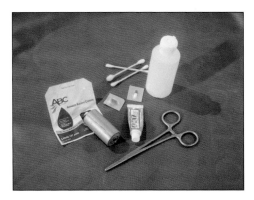

The solution to many canine problems.

Duct tape makes a great boot or bandage, even an emergency leash. Energy goop or snacks will keep his metabolism firing on all cylinders during a long day in the field.

A cotton swab gets most gunk out of eyes, and a hemostat can be used to pull porcupine quills. A multi-tool with scissors solves a multitude of problems big and small for both of you. A small squeeze bottle of distilled water will help wash away dirt in eyes or wounds.

My little bag also contains gauze that will stop bleeding, and an antihistamine to minimize throat-tissue swelling resulting from snake bites.

Hands-Off Training

Electronic collars are to dog training what the TV remote is to most of us: convenient, affordable, and, in practiced hands, effective. They are the equivalent of a canine hearing aid. However, many hunters think they can correct their dogs' every transgression with a push of a button. This is not the case and doing so can ruin a perfectly good hunting dog. Use electronic collars with caution and care to tweak, not stifle, your dog's performance.

I have no idea what he sees, so I won't touch the e-collar transmitter.

There are at least three occasions when I keep my hand off the red button:

1. If you can't see him, don't correct. One never knows what's happening behind that bush or over that hill. He may be on point, working a scent cone, or even coming my way for more direction. Don't ruin your dog with an ill-timed electronic jolt.

2. If my dog's trying to do something, anything, even remotely near what I've asked him to do, I put the transmitter in my pocket. He may only get an "A" for effort, but I don't want to discourage that.

3. When I am not absolutely sure the dog completely understands my command. It may be that his training is incomplete or maybe I can't be heard, but if there's any doubt, I take my thumb off the transmitter button.

And finally, be sneaky when using a transmitter. It's supposed to be magic, a secret. You don't want the dog discovering you are the source of those annoying snaps of electricity. If Buddy ever figured out that I was the keeper of the kilovolts, he'd fear me, period. Keep the transmitter out of sight when you're using it so your dog doesn't put two and two together.

Yes, it may be shocking (pun intended), especially if you're thinking it's the miracle cure to your dog's ills. But there are a lot of times when the smartest move you can make with an electronic collar's transmitter is no move at all—toward the red button.

Be a Good Guest

As a guest in someone else's house, you're expected to be on your best behavior. But, hunt someone else's covert, or hunt with someone else's dog, and everybody becomes a critic. Be a good guest out there, too, and everyone goes home happy. Here are four tried-and-true guidelines.

1. Ask first. Sure, offer to help, but let the dog's owner tell you what to do and when, whether it's feeding, doctoring, or field etiquette. Ask about shooting at wild flushes, or if you can shoot at birds that flush over a broken point.

He didn't deserve that pat on the head, Terry, but it's okay.

2. Bite your tongue. Keep your criticism to yourself. If your dog was performing better, you'd be hunting behind him. Same for commands, which usually have no impact on a dog coming from a stranger. Discipline from you adds little training value and can easily strain a friendship.

3. Help a dog retrieve to his owner by turning away if he comes toward you with a bird. It eliminates confusion and ensures a solid fetch. Most dogs will fetch every bird that falls and return them to his owner no matter who shot it, but there are exceptions. Go with the flow and let the dog handler make the rules.

4. One thing you can almost always do is offer up a "Good dog." A scratch behind the ear, a stroke on the back, or some water from your canteen are always welcome. Ditto for the owner. Don't offer food or treats unless the dog's owner approves.

And don't forget the standard obligation of any sporting guest. A bottle of something old from Scotland presented to your human host is a good way to ensure a return invitation.

Beyond Protein

It's not all about the dogs, the game, even the surroundings (beautiful as they may be). Or maybe it is, if you look at them from a different perspective. But it's my belief that there is a lot more to bird hunting than obtaining protein. Open your eyes a bit more, see things in a different light. Periodically refocus on what's really important to you. Learn as you go, be open to new ideas, and repeat as necessary.

Where else would you find scenery like this?

Go "Unplugged" Sometimes

I love my electronic training collar. It beeps to tell me Manny's found a bird, toots when I need to find him, and even flashes a light as dusk approaches. But when the battery goes dead, magic often results.

After a few steps in the natural quiet, the pulse of an intimate draw can fill your ears. Maybe there's enough snow to muffle your boot steps, but it can't mask the tinkle of a dog's collar tag as he floats nimbly through the sage. Each puff of breeze rattles the dry leaves of mountain mahogany. Maybe it's a song-bird's call you don't recognize. Or a flock-mate's wing beats as it flushes from a nearby juniper, magnified by the lack of background noise from jets and trucks. Once our ears become attuned and alert, our other senses follow.

The play of light on rock and snow almost dances along with us. A looming basalt column grows before your mind's eye. The buckaroo's line shack in pre-topple mode cries out. Crumbling roof boards resembling a crone's mouth, showing more spaces than teeth. That tang assaulting my nose emanates from a plant I can't recall, taking me back to high school and memories of an old girlfriend's perfume.

A hag of an apple tree breathes sickly sweet, its fruit now brown or purple or black, save for one. I flew valley quail at the base of a draw where the ancient cottonwoods stand guard, their flush distilled to the essence of dreams: quivering stalks and crackling leaves, staccato alarm call, drumroll of wings, and lightning-crack gunshots. Their breasts will be accompanied by that one good apple, in a dish I'll cook tomorrow. But, the sights and sounds of the day will live in my mind long after the plates are washed and put away.

Put Your Best Feet Forward

"Walk This Way" is more than an iconic rock tune (the *original* version by Aerosmith). Ambulating with some care husbands your precious energy and may save a trip to the emergency room. Where I hunt in the darkest spot in the Lower 48, I am the farthest anyone can get from a hospital in the contiguous United States. That's as good a reason as any to think before I step.

It starts with minimizing the strain on thigh and calf muscles by stepping around, not over, logs and rocks. Each upward stride is like climbing stairs, taxing some of the largest muscles in your body and lifting virtually your entire body's weight each time you clamber over a downed tree.

If you must negotiate a boulder field or rocky slope, the safest route is through the low spots between rocks. You have less chance of twisting an ankle or breaking a femur because you're carefully, deliberately putting your feet where they'd go anyway in a mishap. Whether rocks are securely anchored or loose as bowling balls is immaterial to your delicate bones and joints.

On steep uphills, conserve energy with a slight rest of your muscles as you lock your knee at the apex of each step. Your legs' skeletal structure supports your body weight for a microsecond, giving oxygen-rich blood a chance to flow back into relaxed muscle tissue. For some reason I tend to stomp on each uphill step, adding injury to the insult of taunting chukars above me. I'm still learning to step lightly instead.

A long day of weaving among the trees and shrubs can be shortened if you weave less. Even if it seems a bit out of the way, walking in longer straight lines (fewer twists and turns) alleviates stress on hip and knee joints and the muscles that activate them. Over the course of a ten-mile hunt, you'll be pleasantly surprised at the absence of pain.

Finally, US Army research shows that shortening your stride just a few inches is wise. Among recruits, it protects against hip and pelvic injuries. This applies to upland bird hunters too. As a bonus, on crusted snow you may find yourself "postholing" less.

At the end of the day, be sure to drink plenty of fluids to replace those expended during your hunt. Muscle cramps are often a consequence of dehydration and constitute one of the most painful late-night "wake-up calls" you'll ever get.

Hunting ... and More!

I've only heard it within the fly-fishing context, but I bet you can make up a hunting version: When first embarking on your journey, you want to catch something, anything, no matter its size. As you progress, you want to catch a lot of fish. Then, your grail is big fish. Ultimately, though, you reach angler's Nirvana and learn to enjoy the trip even if you don't catch any fish.

I won't deny it, I love a full game bag and watching a dog work new cover. When he skids into a rock-hard point and stands trembling, my heart races. If there were a twelve-step program for adrenaline junkies, I'd have to join it.

But I've learned that there is so much more to a hunting trip. Can we better savor the memories of an outing if we stop and smell the (wild) roses? And pine? And juniper? Here are some ways to add additional value to your hunt:

- Look up and down. Appreciate the fall colors, tree-dwelling critters, and those mystifying pawprints in the dust.
- Carry a Ziplock bag for serendipitous discoveries of berries or mushrooms.
- Brew a cup of tea at noon just so you have a reason to stop and breathe deep.
- Bring a non-hunting friend along.
- Spend gas and grocery money near your destination.
- Attend the local hunter's breakfast.

- Donate to the local PTA, Boy Scout troop, or bake sale.
- Visit the state wildlife biologist during the off-season.
- Study the area's ancient history.
- Carry enough coffee (jerky, candy bars) to treat anybody you meet in the field.

Take It with You

There are a number of things I won't leave camp without, things that will ensure I'll probably survive a night or two in an emergency. Without them, my wife will be contacting my life insurance agent posthaste. Most of these items will simply make your hunting day more enjoyable, but others could literally save your life.

I'll carry this stuff any time I can't see my truck:

1. Water for humans and dogs, and a way to purify more. I like a bota bag, which the dog can share. There's minimal loss when squirting water into the dog's mouth.
2. Compass, map, and the knowledge to use them.

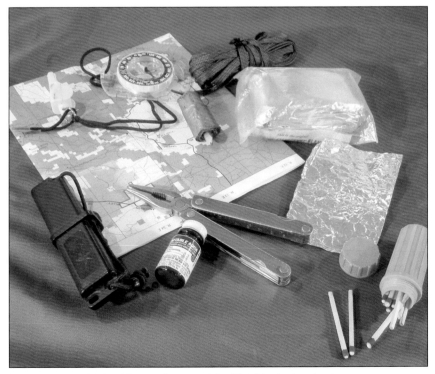

The bird hunter's essentials. The black plastic gizmo
on the left is a Gerber fire starter.

3. Fire starter.
4. Weather protection: space blanket or a plastic garbage bag in a pinch.
5. A whistle (carries farther than a shout for help).
6. Aluminum foil (carries water, can be used for cooking, serves as a signal mirror).
7. Multi-tool.
8. Duct tape (bandages wounds, makes emergency dog boots, and repairs all manner of broken stuff).
9. Parachute cord (makes a bootlace or dog leash, lashes shelter poles).
10. An extra fire starter.

Now, go out and find a bird!

7

Care and Feeding

"Dogs are not our whole life, but they make our lives whole."

—Roger Caras

YOU WOULDN'T IGNORE the check engine light on your dashboard. Nor would you go without changing the oil. Your dog deserves at least as much attention.

Our dogs are elite athletes. They give their all, day in and day out, taxing their bodies as well as their minds. The right care at the right time will keep them healthy and happy, ready to perform the next time you open the crate door and say, "Hunt 'em up."

Check Your Dog Daily

Fall is the best time of year for bird-hunting humans, but it can be the worst time of year for our dogs. Everything out there can cut, bite, sting, scratch, or otherwise damage your best friend. (I remember the first porcupine encounter like it was yesterday!) You can keep minor problems minor, and minimize major problems with a careful examination of your dog after each outing.

Foxtails, cheatgrass, and other weed seeds are some of the worst offenders. They will get in your dog's mouth, eyes, nose, between his toes or pads, and lodge in ears. I know someone who lost a great shorthair to an inhaled foxtail that infected a lung, undiscovered until it was too late to save him. Another wondered why his Springer's foot was swollen until he found a seed burrowed into the skin between toes, abscessed and infected.

"Awns" are the type of seeds (like foxtail) that can burrow into the skin, migrate to internal organs, and kill a dog, so have your pet stand for an inspection after each hunt, ideally immediately following. From puppyhood, get him used to ear poking, toe holding, and eyelid lifting. Pay special attention to the deeper space between a dog's two middle toes.

Even minor cuts and scratches can become infected, so check your dog for blood, watch for persistent licking (often a sign of pain or blood), and dig deep into thick coats for a visual inspection of his skin. Foot pads, especially the accessory carpal pad (a dog's "thumb"), are particularly prone to cuts and bumps.

Other signs something may be wrong include head shaking, favoring one foot or leg, pawing at eyes or ears, and face rubbing on furniture or the floor. If you observe any of these signs, take another look or head for the vet—like the commercial used to say, you can pay the vet now (cheaper) or later (cha-ching).

After all your dog's done for you, a physical exam each day is the least you can do for him.

Familiarity Breeds Contentment

With Buddy, I've learned there are two kinds of conditioning: Getting in shape with regular exercise is the obvious one. The other conditioning is behavioral, i.e., learning something new but necessary. Most of us do a good job with the physical exercise, the field stuff. It's the rest we ignore until it's too late.

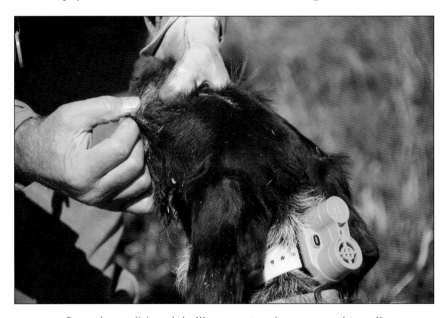

Properly conditioned, he'll cooperate when you need to pull porcupine quills.

Dogs can be flexible beings, but they aren't open-minded and they have a healthy fear of the unknown. Gadgets and unfamiliar actions are anathema to a dog. You don't want to discover that when you're pulling porcupine quills from his nose or when a hunt test judge wants a look at his teeth or your vet suspects there's something in his eye. Each of these could easily turn into a rodeo. But if you've *gradually* exposed your dog to new experiences, he'll breathe deeper and stay calm.

It doesn't matter which situation or piece of equipment we're introducing; any dog learns fastest when you take it one comfortable step at a time.

1. Show him any tools you'll be using, from nail clippers to brushes. If it makes noise, introduce it at a distance, gradually bringing it closer.
2. Let the dog see that the gizmo isn't going to hurt him. Let him smell, taste, and touch it. Use it on yourself (at least, so it appears so).
3. Touch him first where he's most comfortable, gradually working toward your ultimate target. Usually, if he can track it with his eyes, see it touch him, he's less inclined to bolt. To this day, I start all nail trims on a front foot.
4. Reward each forward step. Praise tells a dog everything's all right.

Personal, sometimes invasive procedures will never be a walk in the park, but doctoring, grooming, and such will be less traumatic. The dog will have more confidence in you, no matter what you're doing with—or to—him.

Law of the Pack

There is always a pecking order in the family pack. The question is, who defines it?

All animals, from humans to dogs to cockroaches, function under a "Law of the Pack." In so-called advanced societies, it may not go by that name or be quite as obvious, but there is always a leader and a hierarchy among the subordinates.

Not honoring this genetically coded protocol can cause a heap of trouble when it comes to you and your dog. That's how I learned this lesson . . . the hard way. The details aren't critical to this essay, just the fact that once in a while, two dogs jockeying for lead position will eventually decide the matter with a fang-and-claw debate.

You can likely orchestrate the situation from Day One and nip disaster in the bud. Overtly or covertly, you will probably have to manage the human-dog hierarchy throughout your dogs' lives. Sometimes it's easy, other times, not so. The lessons I learned might help.

"Dominance" doesn't have to mean you physically lord it over your dog(s), or kick, hit, or physically assault your hunting partner. It is as much psychology as anything else. We are supposed to be smarter than our dogs, right? But even mind games sometimes require a little physicality. (Emphasis on "little.")

Dog behavior training begins in the litter. Behaviorist Ed Bailey insists a puppy learns how to "get along"—when to give and when to get—in the last crucial weeks before you pick him up. As long as you don't take him home until the tenth week he should be fine for life. Those last three weeks stretching beyond the traditional forty-ninth going-home day are the pup's finishing school when it comes to getting along with other dogs and, ultimately, with people. I'll let you and your breeder have that discussion.

Once he becomes a member of your family, pup needs to know he is not in charge . . . ever! Whining and crying are his principal weapons, and he will use them to train you. If you're not careful, you will be getting up when he wants out, filling bowls when he wants food, subconsciously petting or jumping off the couch when he craves attention.

Getting along begins with a clear "pack order."

If there are other dogs or humans in the house, the newcomer must understand his place on the totem pole: Rock bottom!

Horses, dogs, humans, chickens . . . all function best and are happiest when they know where they stand, literally and in the pecking order (yep, that's where the term came from—chicken flock dynamics). When you—or the new pup—upset the relationship apple cart, more than fruit will be spilled.

Some clear indications a dog is trying to get a leg up, so to speak, include charging out the door ahead of you or more senior dogs, sitting or standing on your foot, laying a head on your knee or his foot on your foot, lying on the couch or chair—especially in your spot. With two dogs, the dominant wannabe will try to get between you and the other dog, or physically above it (on the couch, for instance, while the other dog lies on the floor).

But be strong, and insist that everyone else in the family grow a pair too. Give your more senior dogs their due and maintain psychological reign over all of them, in hierarchical order.

Cuddly little puppies are smarter than they look. They aren't manipulative, just acting on their natural urges to become the top dog, and ultimately, sire the next generation in their pack. If you persevere and maintain your own leadership status, eventually your dog(s) will accept his role and everyone will get along just fine.

Again, heed my experience. Once a pup is housebroken, out-of-the-crate time is your decision, not his. He'll soon adjust to your timetable. Physically subordinate the new pup to you, family members, and other dogs. My old dog gets to share the couch with me at coffee time. The young one doesn't. He gets the spot at my feet while I gag down a mug of joe.

Young Dog gets fed last, let in and out of the house after Old Dog, and is even trained after Old Dog. When I hunt, Old Dog gets the first "up," and Young Dog is expected to wait patiently for his shift. If Young Dog comes over for scratches and pats, wheedling his way between Old Dog and me, he's pushed away. His place is outside the inner circle.

Yes, it's hard, parceling out attention and affection according to rules of hierarchy, rather than "democracy." But a dog that knows his place in the pack functions better, is more comfortable, and ultimately is a better hunting partner and pet.

Blessed Relief

Every dog has its day, and then at night he's sore and tired. Prescription pain relievers and anti-inflammatories are expensive and dangerous, and often such solutions aren't really called for when Fido simply needs a little help getting to sleep after a hard day afield.

The solution? Plain, old, buffered aspirin. Non-buffered types can irritate a dog's stomach, so use them only as a last resort. Dosage is much greater than most campfire discussions might indicate. My vet recommends 10 mg per kilogram (2.2 lbs.). A typical seventy-pound dog, then, can safely take an average 325 mg tablet twice daily. And just for the record: Products containing ibuprofen or acetaminophen can be harmful to dogs, so stay away from them. To be safe, never give your dog any medication without first clearing it with your vet, who will be the one who has to clean up your mistakes in the long run.

What's Up, Chuck?

Want to save your dog's life? Invest in a bottle of hydrogen peroxide. And not because you can clean open wounds with it (which is usually not the best idea anyway). If your dog is like mine, he'll swallow almost anything he encounters, from garbage to roadkill, rocks, chocolate, socks, and gloves.

Most of these items will eventually pass through, but often it's safer to get it out sooner rather than later. And that means vomiting. Hurling. Tossing his cookies, even if he doesn't want to. If you've figured out what happened within a couple hours, this trick might be the quickest route back to normalcy.

Most of us carry three percent hydrogen peroxide in our first aid kit, so all you need is some way to get it down your dog's gullet. A big syringe or squirt bottle can work. Put a couple of tablespoons of peroxide into the syringe, open his mouth and make sure he swallows. Keep him close, walk him around a bit, and in ten or fifteen minutes, the problem ought to be back on the ground, where it probably began. If not, one more squirt and a little more strolling should do it.

Just like humans, you don't want caustic or sharp materials coming back up through the throat so think twice before using this life-saving trick. But in many cases, hydrogen peroxide can save you an expensive trip to the vet.

After the Hunt

What you choose to feed your dogs is between you and your vet. I'll leave the "Yeah, but" discussions to those who inhabit the online chat rooms. What else you put in your dog's belly, and when, is important enough to bring up here.

A number of studies (on sled dogs and bird dogs) and some long discussions with research vets and field trialers have convinced me that what you do at the end of the hunt day is critical if you want maximum performance from your dog the next day and the next.

Your objective is to give your dog's muscles the cell-repairing glycogen (a carbohydrate) they need. Done consistently, research shows your dog's muscles can experience up to a ninety-five percent recovery rate. Based on current science and practical experience, here's the best way:

Drink up, little guy, for maximum muscle recovery.

1. Immediately after your dog is done hunting (within fifteen minutes) provide water containing maltodextrin (see package directions for dosage). Maltodextrin is a tasteless white powder (a derivative of corn) that a dog's body converts to glycogen. One brand I like is Glycocharge. It's liver flavored and seems to be palatable to a dog.

2. Do not add it to food. The fat in dog food inhibits the uptake of the nutrients in the maltodextrin.

3. Wait at least another hour and a half before feeding.

Unlike humans, dogs shouldn't "carbo load." High-carbohydrate diets can contribute to a condition called "exertional rhabdomyolysis," or "tying up," which causes muscle pain and cramping, watery stool, and dehydration. Hardworking dogs derive much of their readily accessible energy from fat, so fat-heavy and low-volume snacks are better.

Sleeping through the Night

Anyone who brags that their ten-week-old pup sleeps through the night is either a) very lucky; b) hallucinating; or c) not giving their pup enough water. A young dog's bladder simply isn't big enough to retain the fluid his body creates, so it is most likely that he is somewhat dehydrated if he can hold it all night.

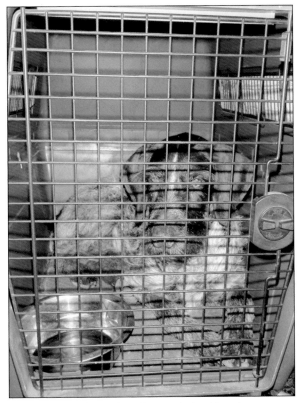

Even a dark-colored crate helps him sleep.

That said, we were getting a good five hours of blissful REM sleep before the whimpering started when Manny was ten weeks old. At twelve weeks, six hours. Eventually we figured out that factors other than bladder capacity were also at work. Maybe these suggestions will help you gain another hour of much-needed rest.

1. Darkness to light: Where I live, the summer sky begins to brighten at about four thirty in the morning. Gaps in the window shades let in that glimmer of sun and soon after, strident puppy voices can be heard. Better window coverings help. But to a remarkable degree, when Manny graduated to a larger, dark-colored crate (with fewer holes and more solid sides), he slept in (everything's relative).

2. Crate size: Not putting your pup in a crate at night? No lectures here about housebreaking, but my experience might be added incentive. A pup needs a cozy "den" he can call his own, but not too cozy. He needs enough room to stretch full length to sleep. Another indicator that the crate is too small: his feet bang up against the sides frequently, waking him—and you.

3. Pick up the water. A tiny bladder stays empty if you don't refill it. Empty the water bowl a couple of hours before bedtime, let him pee immediately before bedtime, and enjoy a few more minutes of slumber.

4. When you pee him, poop him. Or you'll be back outside in another hour. Take my word for it. Bundle up if necessary, be patient once he's out there, and let him take care of business.

5. Lights out when you take him. Like humans, brightening the surroundings sends wake-up signals to the brain that take time to counteract. A flashlight with a red lens cover will help you avoid stubbing toes or knocking over bookcases.

6. Don't let him run, or when really young, even walk, very far to pee. Remember when your kids were young and you were returning from grandma's house? Carrying them from the car to the bed often ensured an uninterrupted snooze. Try the same thing with your new pup.

7. Toys and chewies are great as incentives to go into, and make "crate time" more enjoyable. But when it's sleepy time, eliminate the physical distractions.

I don't have kids, but those who do can add to the list. I look forward to seeing your comments. Right after my nap.

Footsore? Foot Sore?

I hope you'll visit my blog sometime. When you do, you'll find one post that's generated more discussion than all the others. It's about dog boots. You love 'em, and hate 'em. They cost an arm and a leg, so to speak, and seldom last very long if they're not lost first. My solution: duct tape.

A roll of duct tape used for emergency dog boots will last several seasons, making the cost-per-boot mere pennies. When one does come off in the field, you're not mad at yourself or the dog.

Here's how to do it: Tear off a piece of tape that is about a foot long. Some trainers will fit their dog's paw into a baby sock or apply Vet Wrap first to protect the leg hair. My dogs can afford to lose a few hairs, so I don't bother.

Lay the tape on the ground, sticky side up. Put the dog's foot in the middle, and loosely wrap Roman-sandal style (spirally) up and around each foot and lower leg. No need to close off the toe-end; in fact, you want any gunk that gets in to have a way out. If you find the faux boot falling off prematurely, wrap the tape a little higher on the leg so there's more sticky tape surface contacting dog. Go as high on the front foot as the carpal pad, on the back halfway to the "knee."

Check often to make sure you haven't restricted blood circulation. Keep the tape nice and loose all the way up. The wrapping that goes all the way over the fat part of the foot-leg holds the tape on. Practice a few times before your first day in the field unless you enjoy Chinese fire drills. By the end of most hunts, it's possible to just pull off the entire boot.

Routine Feeding

All right, so what do you feed your dog? When? Why?

Any two dog owners will probably yield three opinions on the subject. With the dog food industry constantly changing along with their products, it pays to stay on top of things. Ingredients, formulas, additives—all are worth a long look. Once you decide, consider some things I've learned:

Hunting dogs need protein in their diet, at least thirty percent. In most high protein dog food formulations, fat will usually run in the twenty to twenty-two percent range. Protein is critical as a source of energy for dogs (much as humans need carbohydrates). Some of us feed higher ratios of each, but a discussion with your vet, and careful monitoring of your dog's waistline are in order before you go much above these ratios.

If you ramp up the fat and protein preseason, start feeding the good stuff at least sixty days prior to the first hunt so all the nutrients have time to positively effect muscles, skin, and bone.

Good protein sources include the various fresh meat or fish meals, meaning "real" meat, fish, or eggs. Lower-quality and less-digestible (more waste) versions include meat and chicken byproducts, bone meal, corn, and other grain products. If you find your dog has frequent ear infections or is constantly scratching, look at food allergies as well as the more typical medical causes.

When to Feed

Just as important as what you feed is when you feed. There are simple mechanical reasons not to feed your dog the morning of a hunt. An empty GI tract doesn't hold anything that could rattle around, slowing the dog down and making him want to slip under a low-hanging bush for a nap.

Try this experiment: Take off your sock (representing your dog's stomach and intestinal tract). Drop your car keys (ersatz "dog food") into it. Hold it horizontally, and the dog food will settle in the heel. Then jiggle it, swing it back and forth, whip it around a little like a dog on the hunt might. All that weight will make the sock swing, bounce up and down, perhaps even twist on itself. Veterinarians call it gastric volvulus, a condition that is often fatal.

Your dog's athletic performance is your primary concern. Studies have shown that a dog with food in its gut runs slower, is less agile, and has less stamina than a dog that's hunting on an empty stomach.

Another point. An unfed dog's gut is not using the body's finite amount of energy to digest food when it could be fueling active muscles that are chasing birds.

Avoid guilt trips here by remembering that your dog's metabolism is unlike yours. Sending your dog into the field without breakfast will have no ill effects. Unless he's suffering from other health problems, he won't develop "low blood sugar."

Because dogs get their version of instant energy from fat, if you can't resist giving Gunner something during the hunt, give him a high-fat content snack that won't fill his belly. You can make your own, or simply offer him some of your salami sandwich (just the meat). There are plenty of commercial versions out there in tubes, droppers, and blocks. The key is low volume, high fat to keep his belly as empty as possible.

Water is always welcome.

You can't go wrong with offering water frequently—it keeps a dog cool as well as hydrated. Make life simple on both of you by carrying a bota (wine skin) or the modern equivalent. Teach your dog to drink from it just like you do to make hydration more convenient.

First Aid for Common Hunting Situations

I guess I've got my next book outlined already. It will be a simple, practical handbook on field first-aid for sporting dogs. Based on conversations with hundreds of hunters, it's clear there are simply too many dicey situations for a section in a book that's supposed to be about hunting and hunting dogs. For now, I'll provide a few suggestions for some of the most common and most critical situations. You should probably invest the time in preparing for these, plus more specific situations unique to your area, season, or dog . . . at least until my next book comes out.

Plan Ahead:

A dog that has been introduced to your poking and prodding in advance will be a much more cooperative patient in the field. Practice eye and ear examinations, handling feet, opening and examining mouths. I love my dogs and (I hope) they love me. But they may still bite when they are in pain or afraid. Know how to muzzle and calm your dog to prevent biting. A leash, duct tape, shoelace, or bandanna will substitute for a proper muzzle in a pinch.

Basic First Aid Supplies:

This little kit won't take up much weight or space but it could possibly save your dog's life. Do your best hunting buddy a favor and carry it every time you get far enough from your truck you wouldn't want to carry him all the way back.

- Cotton swabs: cleans wounds, remove seeds from eyes.
- Benadryl or other antihistamine: reduces windpipe swelling from snakebite or insect stings.
- Duct tape: all-around bandage, emergency boot.
- Blood-clotting gauze.
- Triple antibiotic ointment: prevents infection in wounds.
- EMT Gel: stops most bleeding, speeds healing.
- Hemostats: for pulling porcupine quills, foreign objects from wounds and nostrils, etc.
- Phone numbers, hours, and locations of nearest veterinarians.

Critical First Aid Situations and Their Early Responses:

Poisonous Snake Bite

Symptoms (all or none may be observed): a sudden yelp, possibly from fighting with the snake; one or two blood droplets at bite site; swelling of a limb, face, or large lump on body; labored breathing, panting.

Most dogs won't die of a rattlesnake bite, but it is still serious and requires immediate veterinary attention. Cottonmouth, water moccasin, or copperhead bites are more toxic, but are in the same family of pit vipers, so as far as first aid goes the same short-term fixes will help. All suspected snake bites should be treated as serious and your first priority should be getting the dog to a veterinarian as soon as possible. Expect the dog to be out of business for several days, even weeks.
First aid:

1. Separate dog from snake to avoid multiple bites.
2. Calm dog, prevent as much movement as possible until you get to the veterinarian.
3. Administer antihistamine. Open the capsule and place powder under dog's tongue, hold mouth shut a few seconds until dissolved. If you have children's Benadryl, simply pour the solution under the dog's tongue. About 25 mg is the recommended dose for a fifty-pound dog.
4. Carry the dog to the truck, make him lie down.
5. Head for nearest veterinarian.

Cuts, Scrapes, Scratches

Symptoms: You may not see much blood, especially on long-coated or dark-colored dogs. A cut dog may lick one area repeatedly (a common indication of a wound), which may prevent you from seeing blood.
First aid:

1. If bleeding is profuse, pulsing, or the wound is large, cover with clean dressing and apply pressure with your hand until bleeding stops. If you have blood-clotting gauze or EMT Gel, use it. If dressings become soaked, add more but do not remove any. Maintain pressure until you get to a veterinarian.
2. If you can see muscle or bone, get to a veterinarian as soon as possible.
3. On smaller wounds, remove foreign objects, dirt, etc., from the wound with hemostats and cotton swabs. Cleanse wound by rinsing repeatedly with distilled water (any water is better than none).
4. Blot or air dry the wound.
5. Apply triple antibiotic ointment, bandage, and prevent dog from chewing or licking (use Elizabethan collar if needed).
6. If you think the cut needs stitching or stapling, do not apply antibiotic ointment as it speeds the healing process and makes stitching more difficult.

Ear Infections

Symptoms: Odor, waxy substance in ears, head shaking, carrying the head cocked to one side, pain when ears are touched.

First aid: Because this condition has a variety of causes, you may need to experiment. Your best bet is a veterinary exam. Some of the common causes are ear mites and yeast infection (moisture and even diet can aggravate these). Until you can get to a vet, try cleaning the ear with any of the veterinary ear-cleaning and drying substances available over the counter. If you don't have access to them, a fifty-fifty solution of water and white vinegar squirted into the ear, massaged vigorously, and then swabbed out along with the gunk will get things started in the right direction. Continue twice daily until you can get the dog to a veterinarian.

Torn Pads

Symptoms: Limping, licking, or chewing at foot. Bleeding, peeling skin.
First aid: Similar to cuts, above, except:

1. If flap of pad skin is still attached, remove it with clean scissors but do not cut too close to where skin is attached to foot. (Check with your vet before performing this procedure.)
2. After bandaging, apply boot or temporary boot made of duct tape.
3. Prevent dog from running and walking until pad is healed. EMT Gel can speed healing.

Many pad tears occur on the edges of the pad or on the carpal pad (a few inches up the dog's front leg) so check each leg carefully.

Objects in Eye

Symptoms: Pawing or scratching at the eye, rubbing face on ground or furniture, blinking, swollen-looking lid, or odd lump under eyelid.
First aid:

1. Gently pull lower and upper eyelids up or down and examine eyeball.
2. Gently squirt distilled water from outer corner toward inner corner of lower eyelid to wash away any debris. On upper eyelid, use a cotton swab.
3. If that doesn't work, tease a few fibers up from cotton swab. Slowly sweep from outside to inside with a twirling motion to catch hidden debris.
4. If the dog continues to exhibit symptoms after you've removed all the foreign matter, see a vet:

   a. Something may be lodged under the pink tissue behind the lower lid (the "third eyelid" or nictating membrane).
   b. The eyeball or cornea may be scratched or cut.

Be careful what you put in his eye after you remove the gunk. A scratched cornea will be adversely affected by many antiseptic ointments containing steroids.

A veterinarian should be asked to look at any eye injury and recommend treatment options.

Objects in Ear

Symptoms: Head shaking, scratching at ear, rubbing ear on ground or furniture, one ear carried higher than other, head angled to one side.

First aid:

1. Have an assistant hold your dog's head close to his chest with both hands to minimize movement, one hand on muzzle, one behind ears.
2. Examine ear. Many seeds will work their way into the ear canal but can be removed if you catch them early.
3. Use a tweezer or hemostat if necessary, but don't dig more than an inch or so into the ear to avoid puncturing the eardrum. If you don't catch it in time, put a few drops of cooking oil or mineral oil in the ear to help soften the seed until you can get to a veterinarian.

Overheating

Symptoms: Panting that doesn't stop, dog searching for shade or digging a hole to lie in, white gums, confusion, unsteadiness on his feet.

Seeking out shade is a sure sign of a hot dog.

First aid:

1. Get dog to a cool area, such as natural shade, a vehicle with air conditioner on, etc. Aim cool air stream at the dog if possible.
2. Allow sips of water or squirt some from a bota or syringe into dog's mouth.
3. Squirt water or (better) rubbing alcohol on the dog's belly, armpits, chest, and top of head.
4. Do not place dog in an ice bath—it may induce shock.
5. See a vet—serious heat exhaustion can cause brain damage.

Some other external cooling techniques include spraying the dog down with cool water; immersing the dog's body in cool water; wrapping the dog in cool, wet towels; convection cooling a wet dog with fans.

Ticks

Symptoms: Few if any in the field. Conduct a body check to reveal embedded ticks, which may be engorged with blood. Prevention in the form of spray, drop, collar, or tag is worth more than a pound of cure.

First aid:

1. Slip tick-removal tool or the edges of two credit cards between the tick's head and dog's skin.
2. Gently, without twisting, lift the head away from the skin until it detaches.
3. Do not squeeze the tick's body; it could regurgitate toxic stomach contents into your dog.
4. If head detaches from body, use tweezers to remove it.
5. Wash the bite area with antiseptic soap, apply triple antibiotic ointment, and monitor site for telltale "bull's-eye" mark that signals Lyme disease.
6. Search for additional ticks—they travel in packs!

Tick removal tool.

A match, soap, petroleum jelly, or other substance applied to the tick will not induce it to "let go" and may kill it while still attached.

Porcupine Quills

Symptoms: Quills visible (many are not, especially those lodged in gums, tongue, and fur), scratching, licking, head shaking. Quills travel gradually inward and can damage internal organs while moving through the body. It is critical to get them out quickly.
First aid:

1.   Examine the dog's body—search for the shortest quills and pull them first before they migrate under the skin. If you can't get one out in time, mark by cutting the surrounding hair for your vet to remove surgically as soon as possible.
2.   Use hemostat or needle-nose pliers to pull quills straight out without twisting. A quick, sharp motion is better for you and the dog in the long run.
3.   Once you think you're done, re-examine your dog's entire body. I can almost guarantee you'll find more quills in his mouth, ears, and face, between his toes, on his tongue, etc.
4.   Check your dog every day after a porcupine encounter because an undetected quill may migrate to the point you can pull it before it gets stuck in his tongue—or you.

Pouring hydrogen peroxide on quills or cutting off their ends so they collapse have not proven to make removal any easier.

Stomach Twist, Bloat, Gastric Torsion

Symptoms: Bloated or taut belly, restlessness, pacing, a dog that appears to be vomiting without anything coming up, panting. This is a life-threatening situation. Get to a veterinarian immediately.
First aid:

1.   There is a product called Bloat Block that is worth trying while you head for the vet.
2.   Lacking Bloat Block, give your dog some anti-gas medication, such as Gas-X (following your vet's instructions).
3.   Play it safe and don't feed your dog before a hunt.

Swallowed Foreign Objects or Substances

Symptoms: Few, if any. If you suspect your dog has swallowed something, be absolutely sure before taking action. Many smaller items will come back up on their own, usually in the middle of the night. If you suspect your dog has swallowed caustic or acidic substances or sharp objects, do not induce vomiting.

First aid:

1. For small objects that aren't sharp, or materials that aren't caustic or acidic: Squirt 20 cc of hydrogen peroxide down your dog's throat. Walk him around for five to fifteen minutes. Everything should come right up. If not, another squirt and ten more minutes should do it.
2. For fish hooks, feed your dog cotton balls soaked in gravy. With luck they will catch the hooks and move them right through his GI tract. Get him to a veterinarian.
3. For poisons or caustic substances, call a poison control center immediately. If the dog will drink, give milk or water to dilute. Get to the veterinarian.

Poisonous Items Your Dog Shouldn't Swallow (and Their Risks):

Grapes, raisins (kidney failure).

Onions, garlic, leeks (destroys red blood cells).

Chocolate (theobromine causes tremors, seizures, abnormal heart rhythms).

Avocado (contains persin, which is toxic to dogs).

Alcoholic beverages (liver damage, difficulty breathing, coma).

Coffee, tea, caffeine (muscle tremors, bleeding).

Dairy products (diarrhea).

Macadamia nuts (paralysis).

Candy and gum (artificial sweeteners).

Meat fat and bones (cause pancreatitis, choking hazard).

Persimmons, peaches, plums (pits, seeds).

Raw eggs (salmonella, E. coli).

Raw fish ("salmon poisoning," E. coli).

Salt, salty foods (sodium ion poisoning).

Yeast dough (stomach swelling).

If your dog has ingested any of these or other poisonous substances, call your local poison control center or the nearest vet's office.

8

Road to the Utility Test

"I have found it far more pleasurable pursuing the game with a fine dog and enjoying his performance than the actual shooting."

—Robert G. Wehle

THE NORTH AMERICAN Versatile Hunting Dog Association (www. navhda.org) has developed a very practical, comprehensive and well-thought-out testing system for hunting dogs. If your dog can pass the highest-level Utility Test, you have a very good hunting dog. The test includes a combination of skills and abilities, evaluation of key conformation attributes, and obedience, all of which very accurately determine how good an all-around hunting companion your dog is.

I've promised every dog I've owned to help him pass a Utility Test, but something has always stymied us: Calendar, injury, work obligations . . . maybe you know what I'm talking about. With my two-year-old Manny, I'm hoping to work through the roadblocks and deliver on that promise. I even started blogging about it to keep myself honest and on track. The following are excerpts from that chronicle. Whether you're a NAVHDA member, own a versatile dog or not, I hope you will learn from what we've discovered so far about preparing for this challenge:

Looking Downrange

"Easier said than done" is more than a cliché. A dog that passes, let alone earns a Prize I in the Utility Test would be a worthy hunting companion anywhere, anytime, on any game. And that's the challenge. As each new year gets rolling, so do we.

Training, of course, is critical. This is not a test of fundamental natural ability. That train leaves the NAVHDA station at age sixteen months. From flawless retrieves to a civilized partner in the blind, a dog must do it all exceptionally well.

Hunting skills are important in these tests, but poise is also critical. A dog must be cool and calm when necessary, and then be able to kick in the afterburners when the judges say, "Let him go." Add an amoeba-like gallery and a gaggle of other dogs waiting their turn, and it becomes a test of any dog's self-discipline.

Manny was cool and collected from Day One. On his first visit to the vet, he occupied the high ground of the exam table like it was his mountain castle, lying down and crossing his front legs while surveying his new territory like a just-crowned monarch. But as with everything, only practicing for a test will be good practice for a test. I hope to recruit a crowd of helpers-observers.

Water is another story. Few of my wirehairs have had what some call "water love." This is partially my fault, because here in the desert it's hard to find enough water for training purposes. The pup will swim the English Channel to retrieve a bird, but in front of judges? We'll have to wait and see. Sustaining a duck search for ten minutes will be as much an endurance test for Manny as it will be an emotionally wrenching ordeal for me. I almost lost Buddy to a long water retrieve a couple seasons ago and will do everything I can to avoid a repeat.

One of the problems that my career may have exacerbated is Manny's steadiness on flushing birds. For two seasons on my TV show he's been allowed to break at shot and start his retrieve. Now, I'll have to work toward rock-steadiness from flush to shot to fall.

There is an obedience component to this test as well. Steadiness at the blind in the face of multiple gunshots and dropping birds is one example. We also have to walk a short obstacle course at heel. And our nemesis in the Natural Ability Test is cooperation after Manny picks up a bird. He's required to bring it right back, without passing "Go" or collecting $200. (As opposed to deconstructing it in front of three patient judges as he did in his first test!)

No aspect of the NAVHDA test is easy. Dogs—and humans—have good days and bad days. I think I'm ready for the unavoidable natural and human-caused goofs that are out of our control. It's the other ones I'll be preparing for.

Back to the Basics

The "V" in NAVHDA stands for versatile, which in many cases is synonymous with retrieving. As the saying goes, "Conserve game, hunt with a trained dog." That dog must bring back anything you shoot, wherever it lands, every time. (In Europe, and even some NAVHDA tests, furred game can be part of the retrieving challenge, so rabbit and varmint hunters also take note.)

We've got a long way to go, Manny and I. The Utility Test is complex and in large part composed of skills that are difficult to master. They are difficult because they require water and most of us don't have access to the right kind of water. For that reason, many otherwise capable dogs are lacking in this critical component.

So, to the water we went. Luckily, Bob Farris, trainer and NAVHDA judge, was willing to offer some tips. I spent part of my summer vacation working with Farris. To say it was eye-opening would be an understatement.

As most pointing-breed owners ultimately figure out, their dog will pick up and bring back some things sometimes, but "natural retriever" is not a term that applies to us. Force fetch training must be part of our regimen if we're to live up to the "conserve game" credo.

Retrieving in all its forms is a major focus of the test. Manny is not quite at the top of his game due to my lack of diligence. His force training was good, to a point. But on birds, he'd often slack off prior to delivering to hand: stop, drop, or do a little dance prior to delivery. And I'd been remiss in requiring prompt completion of the transaction.

So, back to the training table and yard work. We began with the "Here" command, expecting full compliance no matter the distraction. We started using the back-off, run-away method when necessary, ear pinch as required, augmented

with electronic collar tones, adding the "Fetch" command, and expecting full compliance with that last, crucial ten feet of delivery to hand, finally including water in the equation.

But no birds yet. Bumpers, sure. But I'm not ready to risk a slip of the finger on the red button while birds are in play.

Thanks, Bob. I'll let you know how it goes.

Complete a retrieve—back off as he approaches.

Flush-Flap-"Whoa" Training

"Hope for the best, but plan for the worst," while not originally coined for dog trainers, is a worthy axiom, especially when teaching steadiness to wing, shot, and fall. Every step, every cracked twig or ruffled wing feather is the devil's invitation to Manny, as if the bird were saying, "C'mon, pup, I dare you to flush me."

In getting a dog ready for a fall Utility Test, this may be the ultimate bugaboo. With those two television seasons of solid points and backs, and then "alley-alley-oxen free" when the bird flew, I'm unteaching as much as teaching.

I like the general idea of centering the dog's steadiness training on stop-to-flush. It seems to be the method of choice for my online and in-life friends who train a lot of dogs. But more importantly, it embodies the entire best-worst philosophy. Ultimately, every bird flies. If that act is the command for "Whoa," how can you go wrong? (If anyone can, I'll figure out how.)

Several trainers I respect start with the concluding portion of any command ("Hold," and then proceed with the retrieve, for example). The flush idea corresponds nicely to this. Then, everything leading up to the "Whoa"-to-flush becomes natural, building up to a skill that has previously been mastered.

Manny is already a staunch pointer. It's the next steps that will need diligence on both our parts.

Live and Learn

I once took a music lesson from a master cello player. Somehow we began discussing when he evolved from "cello student" to "cello teacher." He spoke slowly and deliberately in his heavily accented English: "I've never stopped being a student." Nor should dog trainers.

One of the best reasons to attend events like Pheasant Fest is the seminars. Watching experts, absorbing their expertise, soaking in their freely bestowed knowledge, finally "getting it," is worth the price of admission. And that's before the exhibits, meeting friends new and old, and the generally positive vibe you get hanging out in a setting where 22,000 people love what you love.

Sometimes, it's brand-new information that resets your preconceived notions. Other times, it is as simple as a crystal-clear interpretation of a muddy word that unlocks a cascade of training revelations. Long ago I decided that even one nugget, a scintilla of useful information made sitting in a seminar for an hour worthwhile, but Ronnie Smith's recent overview of dog training and behavior provided a headful of invaluable insights. I vowed to use his techniques and tools to prepare Manny for his next Utility Test.

In Ronnie Smith's case, it was using the half-hitch on a dog's flank to reinforce "Whoa." His rationale and method for stopping dogs via flank-based

Rick and Ronnie Smith's half-hitch.

commands resonated in the room of avid dog owners and hunters, many vexed by the lack of success with collar-based direction-correction (including me).

The Hitch, Part Two

In the NAVHDA Utility Test, a dog must be steady to wing, shot, and fall. A recent sad story from Illinois drove home the advantage of a dog that doesn't bolt at the shot. Add the basalt cliffs we hunt for chukars to the test requirement and I'm a believer. Getting Manny there will be a challenge.

But the half-hitch Rick and Ronnie Smith espouse may as well be attached to a magic wand. Unlike the Smith's neck-oriented "point of contact" for going with or coming to you (as they say), it is put to the flank for standing still—"Whoa." You may as well have nailed my dogs' paws to the "Whoa" table for as much movement as they demonstrated. I got a little cocky and hitched both dogs in a point-honor scenario and the magic rope solidified each without an inkling of temptation to dishonor the bracemate. This was also true on retrieves. Each dog watched calmly as the other brought a pigeon to hand.

I know better than to draw too many conclusions from a weekend of experimentation. But so far, thumbs up.

Minor Victories

We are making progress in our training. Manny and Buddy—a team again—are getting steadier by the day. After three days:

1. Flanking the "Whoa" table, with Rick and Ronnie Smith's half-hitch-waist-rope "point of contact," the dogs were attentive and still when the pigeon was fluttered, flapped, and waved in front of them. Not too close, but closer than usual. Ditto when brought downwind of a launcher. They stood side by side (actually, Buddy gets first position, Manny learns manners).

2. Retrieves are also more than simple fetching drills now. Each honors his bracemate, learning patience and additional manners.

3. Next day, the rope was simply draped over their flanks, a tap reinforced the point of contact but no waist wrap. Birds flap, steady again. An earnest, purposeful "duck search" on dry land for the younger dog followed, with a soft-mouthed retrieve after a momentary point upon discovery of the pigeon.

4. Third day: No rope, no table. Dogs loose in the yard. I showed the pigeon and they froze. Big waves, major flaps, up-close-and-personal. Just a tap on their flank and the dogs stood like statues.

Now, of course, I've probably jinxed it.

Through the Decoys

I'm not much of a duck hunter. Sitting in a blind is not my idea of a good time. But my preferences don't matter. Manny must present his duck-hunting chops to win at the NAVHDA Utility Test.

He's required to successfully complete a "duck search," combing brushy water for a frantically escaping-hiding duck. He's got to stand or sit still while shots ring out across a duck pond, eventually swimming through bobbing decoys to make a strong retrieve. So, I've dusted off my floaters and silhouettes and started acquainting the youngster with faux fowl.

He's shown little interest in the plastic phonies while retrieving most everything that I've placed in, around, or beyond the blocks. His uncle, on the other hand, has retrieved several decoys to hand. Maybe he's just trying to be helpful.

We've only just begun, and our work has been restricted to dry land, a far cry from a full string of floating dekes, plus gunshots, a real dead duck, and a gallery of fellow test takers and judges. We're keeping our fingers crossed.

Honor the Retrieve

Backing, honoring—whatever you want to call it—there are at least two techniques I am familiar with. The most common scenario is where one dog points and the other dog glides into a pseudo-point behind the first dog. Eventually, Manny and I will get to that.

I'm beginning to think the *other* type of honoring teaches self-discipline, control, and maybe even a better retrieve. As you know, we've been working on one dog watching, waiting patiently while his bracemate brings back bumpers and other stuff. But lately we've been using real birds, and it's having the desired effect.

Both Buddy and Manny are more energetic on their runout to the bird, lusting for feathered prey. But (luckily) they are each disciplined enough to execute the command, and there is the envy factor: "Gee, if I don't get it, he will." It's a test of wills for all three of us.

So far, so good. It's not in any NAVHDA test until the Invitational, but I'm wondering if the simple act of deferring to another dog (in addition to the human) adds another layer of complexity and thus, perhaps, challenges their intellect.

Put a Hitch in His Get-Along

Of all the things my friend Bob Farris (NAVHDA judge) pointed out on a recent visit, the most gratifying was how steady Manny was on flying birds. Not rock-steady, of course, but better than he was at many of the other aspects

Bob Farris' gut hitch—a check cord can be attached.

of the Utility Test. And I'm confident he'll get better, especially with the help Farris offered us.

Farris acquainted me with his version of the "gut hitch," a variation on Rick and Ronnie Smith's half-hitch around the dog's waist. The basic concept is that a dog will stop—and stay stopped—when he feels pressure on his flank. The hitch applies it.

Farris's rig goes from around the dog's waist to his collar, attaching at both points. A check cord is clipped to the hitch, giving the handler an easy way to apply pressure to the flank from a distance and to the side of the dog. A tug, particularly upward, stops most dogs in their tracks. The advantage to Farris's version is the dog need not drag the entire cord, just the hitch portion, which remains off the ground and attached to his waist and collar. When you want to steady him, simply attach the check cord and tug.

No, it's not quite that easy, but the proper tools make the job a little easier. Now, to put theory into practice.

Tricks of the Trade

I summarized to my wife the biggest challenge of a NAVHDA Utility Test this way: you must train to the test, and you must use tricks to combine the skills needed for each portion of the test. It's no wonder NAVHDA offers handler's clinics, because most of us may never understand the training challenges of this complex series of events unless broken down into components by trainers wiser than we, and then approached in those bits and pieces. Whether you train for NAVHDA or not, the lessons to be learned could be of value in any venue.

The skills and thus tricks are not the obvious A-to-B-to-C string. There is a considerable amount of dog psychology and cheerleading required in getting from start to finish. Understanding what really counts is a lot easier when you can pick the brains of experienced mentors.

The duck search is my current nemesis. Problem number one, the test dog doesn't instinctively know there's a bird in the water somewhere. You must convince him of that, and then chain that to

First goal: get him from here to the other side.

the expectation that he must seek it out and bring it back. Thanks to Farris, I now have a series of exercises designed to prepare him for the task.

Lucky for me, Manny is bird crazy. Farris used that trait to link the components of a successful duck search starting from square one. First objective: send the dog to the far bank of the pond, where any search should begin, so that, with practice, all of the water may be covered. That skill is still a few steps from where we are but it's coming together.

For now, we begin with a swim for a visible, obvious bird in the water. Next, we get Manny to swim farther for the bird, which may not be visible at a distance. If needed, add the incentive of a rock splash when intensity lags. Continue with a bird thrown beyond the rock splashes to convince the dog that it's worth his while to swim all the way across the pond.

In the next phase of the test, the dog is stationed well back from the water, possibly behind the truck, but we make sure he knows there will be a bird waiting for him before he's taken away. Eventually, we'll add a track on the far bank to get Manny to search not just in the water but along the shore as well. If necessary, I'll have someone on the far bank encourage him verbally, possibly tossing a rock or two if he needs direction. With the confidence of knowing there is a bird in there, we hope he will maintain the motivation to search high, low, and in between for the required ten long minutes on test day.

Instinct to Obedience

My eyes have been opened so wide on this aspect of training, I'm going to need Visine! Of the many things I've been enlightened about during the dog training process, steadiness while on birds is perhaps the most useful to me. Maybe it will be of use to you.

We all have our methods for teaching staunchness. Barrel, table, half-hitch, collar, place board, winch, tow truck. All have merit. But those are merely practical applications of a theory I'd never quite grasped.

Think about the temptation, the challenge, the many genetic motivators a dog has for breaking point. In the wild world, a point is merely a pause prior to pouncing on prey—just watch a coyote working a field for mice. Sure, we can stretch the length of that pause in our domesticated dog, but at some point we must overcome instinct alone or he *will* pounce.

As a judge, Bob Farris is asked to evaluate every piece of the point-flush-shot-fall-retrieve process. There are different goals for each, the most important being the separation of instinct (the moment a dog smells the bird and points) from cooperative obedience (when he's commanded to hold that point).

Knowing there are two distinct parts, Farris breaks the sequence into those components: 1) the reactive point (instinct); 2) staunchness (obedience).

He's just acknowledged
my presence . . .

With the "Whoa" command,
he's in obedience mode.

That's how they're judged in a NAVHDA Utility Test, because it's a good way to ensure reliable performance in the field, the goal being a dog that's steady to wing-shot-fall.

Manny is catching on . . . now to get his handler to do the same. Calling on his hunting DNA, the dog is learning that a whiff of bird equals point. But he's also learning that once I'm in the picture giving the "Whoa" command, instinct is out, obedience is in. Eventually, the verbal command will become a hand signal, and then simply a look. By then, the dog should understand that a human walking to the bird means the same thing as "Whoa." A hand signal, the sound of boots scuffed on the ground, a gunshot or long whistle are all part of the "Whoa" command and should be interpreted by the dog as: do not move!

We love our dogs for their instinctive skills and how we share them in the hunt, forming a team that is stronger than either individual. There are plenty of times when the dog's instincts make all the difference. At other times (in training or competition) obedience and cooperation must trump those genetic signals.

The Right Order

Thanks to my lack of foresight, Manny backslid on the one part of retrieving on which we weren't solid: real bird brought to hand without tenderizing it. Recently, his retrieves were energetic and enthusiastic. Using my Real Bird Bumper®, he was scooping, making a U-turn, and racing back with a lusty, throaty growl of pleasure. When a pigeon was substituted, the wheels came off. Thankfully, I figured out why in record time.

Immediately before our retrieving drills we'd been working on steadiness. Manny was confronted with more temptation than he could handle: close-quarter birds flapping and flying in front of a young dog that had been too long in the kennel while I was out of town. The adrenaline was gushing in torrents in Manny's little doggy body. When the retrieving practice commenced a few minutes later

crunch went the bird.

It took one night of fitful sleep before the revelation hit me: divorce flushing, flying live birds from our retrieving . . . for a while. Trainers have had

Break the connection, ensuring a stauncher point.

a corollary drummed into their thick skulls for years: training a dog to expect a retrieve upon every flush (or every shot, for that matter) is folly. The worse your shooting skills, the deeper you sink into that mire. Manny has shown me that the less mature a dog, the farther apart flushes and retrieves should be, literally. Following that session we put some time—and distance—between the two skills.

The strategy worked. I'm still playing it safe, putting my pigeons in the loft after they clock out on their flushing job. Our retrieving work will be limited to Real Bird Bumpers® with chukar wings taped on. They are real enough for now.

Get Along, Get in Shape

It's funny how you think you're doing pretty well in the fitness department, but then with a jolt, you're reminded that you're not as buff as you had thought.

I know I've got a long way to go before my pants are loose and knees less stressed from the extra weight I carry. Let's get that out of the way once and for all. But this also applies to Buddy and Manny. They are magnificent, mystical hunting machines, fine-tuned and perfectly built for their purpose. But my wife remarked today at how Buddy is looking slimmer. Ever slow on the uptake, I finally noticed too. You know how it is, when you've lost a belt-hole's worth of weight, everyone compliments you. Left unsaid is that your previous flabby condition was noticeable, too, i.e., they discerned a difference between your heavy persona and your (usually temporal) less-heavy version. My wife is jealous of how easily I can lose weight until I remind her that, in the offseason, I usually find it again.

All of this made me think that all these months of running one dog and then the other to avoid confrontation effectively halved the length of each dog's workout. Yesterday's long romp among the rimrock and bunchgrass drove home that point. Manny's tongue was dragging, and Buddy was walking alongside me for the last half mile or so. Me? Well, if I could walk alongside myself I would, and my tongue would be dragging in the volcanic dust we call soil here in the high desert.

We could all use more such vigorous workouts. It bodes well for next hunting season, but also for the simple, thirty-minute bit of fieldwork included in Manny's Utility Test. Adrenaline, stimulus overload, and his handler's stress will amp up his average speed, and having a little bit extra in the tank will serve him well.

Thankfully, when daylight saving time is in effect the longer days mean longer workouts, and we plan to take advantage of them.

Shot Equals Stop

Along with the other things we're practicing, Manny is now learning that a gunshot means "Whoa." Yep, I sometimes shoot birds that fly wild, nowhere near my dogs, especially on a slow day, the first day, the last day, or any day when adrenaline is flowing faster than skill and technique. If and when I actually

Hopefully the dogs will "Whoa" and Tad will get some usable footage!

hit something, I want my dogs to be able to find it.

Also, by stopping to the shot (or a flush, a command, or a whistle) Manny and Buddy may actually see the bird drop. If not, at least they are ready for the "Fetch" command and a hand signal assist to the general area. When a chukar tumbles among the rockfall, I like to think they appreciate the heads-up, literally.

In the NAVHDA Utility Test, there are several instances where a shot-equals-"Whoa" sequence will come in handy, such as after pointing birds in the field, but also when standing at the duck blind, watching birds fly and hearing shots from several directions. The duck search also includes a shot and a pause prior to sending him to the water.

As an aside, I've found many uses for a long whistle as another "Whoa" command, much like the retriever trainers use. Last night, Manny did me proud—150 yards from me, he locked up tight when I trilled. Good boy!

In Search of Water

Believe it or not, here on the desert we have a lot of water. Irrigation canals, stock ponds, trout streams, and, if you head for the hills, alpine lakes. But finding a suitable body of water for the Utility Test is a tall order. It must be a good acre or more in surface area and deep enough for swimming. More importantly, it should contain brush, reeds, and other cover for a swimming duck to hide in and a searching dog to work through. Therein lies the rub.

The Natural Ability Test required Manny to simply swim after a bumper twice. I sought permission to use a couple of nearby ponds and a puddle on local BLM land that held enough water during most of the training season. But they all reflect their desert environment in that they are sterile: no brush, no cattails. The Duck Search portion of the test requires ten minutes of aggressive work among the reeds and rushes, mainly while swimming. Of course, no self-respecting rancher wants that stuff in his stock tank.

I'm asking around, getting a few leads. One of my training club members has a line on a marshy patch of a trout stream that may work. A friend has a neighbor who built his own "technical pond" for retriever training. I'm hoping it has brushy edges and that I'll get invited. Google Earth might be of use identifying others. Other dog club members may be of help. I hope. Perhaps the local Soil Conservation Service officer may be able to help.

Minor Victories, Part Two

I'm not bragging, and telling you this might jinx next week's training, but every baby step forward is worthy of celebration around here as we head toward a NAVHDA Utility Test.

One key element of this grueling test is steadiness, not just to a flushing bird but to the shot and the fall. Only when the handler commands a retrieve is the dog allowed to move. This could well be our Waterloo, so it's our training priority these days.

Steadiness has many benefits in the field. Like virtually every component in the test, there's a practical side. Think about your own experience in the uplands: birds that flush over a cliff, wildly flushing birds that you shoot at anyway, bad shots and missed birds, a bird in the air without a point. A dog that will "Whoa" at those moments is a safe dog, ready to make a blind retrieve or hunt on.

So these days, it's "Whoa" training in all its manifestations: at the shot, at a long whistle, with a hand signal and voice. But we also strive for steadiness to the flush, be it bumpers, sticks, and rocks, or while kicking around in the brush for live birds.

The bragging reference? We've had a strong week of training success, including today, which sums up the week. Cross-country we went to avoid all the rude townies clogging our trails. Manny coursed the sage and bitterbrush prairie behind our place with one eye on me, the other on the far horizon. Over the course of the hour, I emptied a blank pistol's eight-shot cylinder to repeated solid stops by Manny. Whistles at a distance, same result. Hand signals, stop. Combinations, more stops. A few retrieves to sweeten the pot were also preceded by one of the "Whoa" signals, and deliveries to hand.

I'll shut up now. No sense in tempting fate. We seem to be on our way.

"Whoa!" And I Mean It

Electronic training collars have many uses, but until recently I avoided using one around birds like a dog avoids baths. But once you figure out that steadiness on birds is a two-part process, your outlook might change. Mine did. First, a dog instinctively slams into a tail-stiffening point. That part, we all get. A whiff of bird scent or sight of a bird should take care of that unless your dog's pedigree included a cardboard box and a hand-lettered You Pick sign.

The second part of the sequence (steadiness) is where I've just become enlightened, thanks again to Bob Farris, trainer and NAVHDA judge. In the Hunt Test judging process, the point is the first stage of judging—i.e., does the dog have the genetic programming to point when prey is upwind of him? But the judging criteria change the moment the dog sees you in the picture, literally or figuratively. That is where the canine rubber meets the obedience road.

Manny (and I'd bet all "finished" dogs) needs training to stay on point until I want him to a) see the bird drop, getting ready for the retrieve; or b) continue to hunt after my release because I missed the bird. When he enters a scent cone, Manny assumes an elegant point, leg up and forward a bit. But a few moments of staring at the source of enticing smell (a walking or fluttering bird or—worse—a flushing bird) will test any dog's resolve. It's a dog's instinct to chase, so the key is making it clear he's been ordered to stand still.

Some trainers use the usual verbal or hand signal. Some transition to a secret-code heel shuffle or other noise or gesture that field trial judges sometimes overlook. I'm figuring that for us the key is treating that part of the point-steady drill for what it is: an obedience situation. Until this revelation, I was loath to use any enforcement stronger than a check cord, gut hitch, or tap on Manny's flank. I feared an electronic collar might sour a dog to birds—especially if I had to use it often.

But if he's been thoroughly drilled in "Whoa" with many and different combinations, live birds simply become just another distraction from the command he knows so well. Tempting, sure, but just a sidebar to an obedience test. Now

that I've gotten him over that, we've made some quantum leaps.

So far, Manny's only been lit up (gently) a couple of times. These days, merely seeing me holding the transmitter is enough to keep him steady on point, despite having birds flapping in his face, covey flushes at his feet, even birds perching on his back. Twice recently we had flawless training sessions. Tomorrow, who knows? But I feel as if we're on the right track.

The sight of the transmitter can help steady him.

9

Skills Every Bird Hunter Should Have

"If you get to thinking you're a person of some influence, try ordering somebody else's dog around."

—Will Rogers

I'LL NEVER FORGET watching someone's tent bouncing its way across the blustery desert because the guy ropes were tied with granny knots. It was another reminder of the practical value of basic outdoor skills. Spending a chilly night under the stars was probably a valuable lesson to that hunter!

As with most things in life, there is usually a right way to perform a sporting task, and a number of wrong ways to do it, and then redo it. Even if you were a Boy Scout, useful skills and indispensable knowledge have a way of getting lost in your mental filing cabinet. Some of them could save a life or avert serious injury. Others are simply helpful and will make your day afield—or training your dog—more productive or enjoyable.

Fire

Nothing caps the day like a bright, cheery campfire. Building one that lights quickly, doesn't smoke, and burns a long time is not difficult if you start with the right ingredients and a little fundamental knowledge.

Unless you plan to signal the International Space Station, a small- to mid-sized fire (a couple of feet in diameter) is plenty for warming, cooking, and camaraderie.

To begin, search out three kinds of burnable material: tinder, kindling, and wood for fuel. Tinder is any flammable material that is dry and small in diameter. Leaves, grass, twigs, and some types of bark are common examples. If you can crush it in your hand and it crunches, it's probably good tinder

Kindling is pencil-diameter woody material four to twelve inches long, including twigs, small branches, and slivers from larger pieces of wood. I like my kindling to have "edges" as opposed to all rounds. Edges seem to better catch the flame from the tinder, giving the fire somewhere to start. A couple of good handfuls of kindling should suffice.

Fuel wood is anywhere from an inch to a foot in diameter. Downed branches and pieces of split logs are common. A foot or two in length is plenty.

Clear an area down to mineral soil and build a two-foot circle of stones to contain the coals. Don't build a fire under overhead branches that could be lit by a wind-blown spark or drip rain or melted snow onto the fire. Then, consider your choice of architecture. I like the "modified log cabin" style of architecture: Two fuelwood "walls" forming a right angle, a big ball of tinder nestled in the corner. Kindling is laid against the walls over the tinder, and a few pieces of fuel wood may be placed above it all. Leave plenty of room for air—a smokeless fire is equal parts heat, fuel, and oxygen. Touch a match to the tinder, and get out the marshmallows.

Orienteering

While a GPS unit can be a lifesaver, map and compass skills will bail you out when batteries fail or no satellites are flying by. At a minimum, know how to identify (and remember) landmarks that will lead you back to a known location.

You should at least learn how to find a "catchline."

Study and then carry a copy of a map of the area you plan to hunt. Make note of a stream, road, ridgeline, or other long, relatively straight feature in relation to where you park or make camp. That's your catchline. You will hunt away from that location, but as long as you know which direction you went in relation to the catchline, you're home free.

Example: I'm camped along a river that runs north and south. I hunt away from camp to the east. When I want to head back, I simply walk west until I reach the river. Camp is either left or right along my catchline. If I'm really smart, I've overshot camp on purpose (say, to the north) so I know to walk south when I hit the stream.

Sharpen a Knife

Any number of gadgets or gizmos will help you put a keen edge on your pocketknife until you're stuck in the woods with nothing but an oily whetstone and a knife that won't cut open a candy wrapper. You can put a pretty good edge on your knife by using your finger as the guide to a good blade angle.

Grip the knife, extending your index finger along the "spine," or top edge of the blade. Try for a ten- to fifteen-degree angle of blade to stone. For field use, the key is maintaining the same angle for both sides of the blade—note where the spine lies in relation to the pad of your index finger.

If you have sharpening stone oil, use it. It keeps friction (and blade-damaging heat) to a minimum. Be generous, because it also carries away the bits of stone and blade that can gum up the sharpening process. Water or saliva will do in a pinch.

On the rough grit side of the stone, make about a dozen strokes with moderate pressure on the blade. Stroke as if you're trying to shave a bit of the stone off. Move the blade in one direction across the stone, not back and forth. Swap hands, check your finger-spine angle, and repeat for the other side of the blade.

Turn the stone to the fine grit side, oil it up, and repeat the process. For most upland uses, that'll do.

Tell Time

Who wears a watch these days? Unfortunately, the modern digital version (mobile phone) sometimes dies when you need it most. If getting back to camp before dark is your priority, figuring out when the sun will set is critical.

Extend your arm to full length, palm perpendicular to the ground. Cock your wrist so you can see your palm with fingers stacked atop each other. Don't look directly at the sun, but focus on your fingers as you raise your hand until your index finger is just under the bottom of the sun. Count the number of fingers between the bottom of the sun and the horizon (if you're lucky, you'll need two hands' worth). Each finger is about fifteen minutes of remaining daylight.

Every finger is roughly fifteen minutes of daylight.

Take Photos and Video

We're not talking art here, simply better snapshots or home movies. If you want to make a statement, go to film school. If you want decent shots to share with friends, read on.

The rules for great photos are simple: Fill the frame. After a few establishing shots to create a sense of scale (tiny guy at the foot of mono-lithic cliff), set up your shots so they are pretty much full of your subject: hunter holding bird, dog with bird in mouth, two guys high fiving. Leave out most of the background unless the background is what you want.

I love this photo, but have never used it. Can you see why?

Most shots are more attractive to the eye if they are a bit asymmetrical. Put the main subject just a bit to the left, right, or toward one corner, up or down. Remember that with most point-and-shoot cameras you'll have to focus on your subject before you decenter it. In most cameras this is done by pushing halfway down on the shutter release while pointing the lens at the subject. Often, the object being focused on is surrounded by a graphic frame in the viewfinder.

Eliminate extraneous, distracting stuff, including cigarettes, soda cans, gear, people in the background and anything in the background that looks as if it's growing out of your subject's head, such as a tree trunk, telephone pole, or fishing rod. The same goes for items in the foreground. For example, I was recently given a set of photos that show a woman's head popping out of my belly!

Hold dead game with a bit of respect.

Shoot at least one "insurance" frame—or more—just in case. Light changes, the flash works (or doesn't), eyes blink, dogs sneeze. Take several images from different angles by walking around the subject. Also, kneel or lie down and take photos from a lower perspective rather than the typical "grip and grin" formatting. In the newspaper business we used to say film is cheap compared to resetting the shot, and now digital bytes are even cheaper.

Videos look more professional if you frame the action and hold the camera stock-still. A tripod, monopod, shooting stick, or anchor of any kind (even leaning against a tree trunk) is better than no support. Avoid following your subject with the camera by literally walking behind or alongside him. Let him walk into and out of the frame instead. Minimize zooms as well. If you want your subject to talk to the camera and be understandable, get close enough so the onboard microphone can pick up his voice. If you must "pan" or "tilt," (move camera horizontally or vertically) take it slow.

Jump-Start a Truck

It's surprising how many hunters don't know how to do this. First, determine if the battery is really dead. If you hear nothing but a "click" when you turn the key, you're likely out of juice. If the motor cranks when you turn the key, it's not a dead battery (but will be soon if you continue cranking without the engine starting).

Point the rescue vehicle nose-to-nose with the one that won't start. If not, figure out where the batteries are on both vehicles, and pull alongside the correct fender. Turn off both vehicles.

Connect the red cable to the positive terminal on the dead battery (look carefully at the battery to make sure it's the positive terminal). Then connect the other end of the same red cable to the positive terminal of the good battery.

Connect one of the black (negative) cable clamps to the negative terminal of the good battery. Then connect the other end to a clean, unpainted, metal surface under the disabled car's hood. Good locations include the manifold, frame (if you scrape the paint off), or any large bolts. Route the cables to ensure they won't tangle in the engine fan, belts, etc.

Start the truck that has the good battery and let it run for a couple of minutes, and then try starting the other vehicle. If it won't turn over in a couple of tries, wait while the "good" vehicle runs a few more minutes and try again. Once the offending vehicle has started, remove the cables in reverse order (avoid letting clamps touch each other unless you like fireworks) and let the jumped car run for at least thirty minutes to ensure that it now has a good charge. Don't turn the engine off again until you arrive at a service station or other place where help is available in case the battery fails again.

Cook a Game Bird

Generally speaking, game birds should be cooked fast and hot; rare is a good plan. Birds will continue cooking once removed from heat, and an overcooked bird is invariably dry and tough. An overcooked duck or goose becomes "fishy," or tastes like liver. Whole birds seldom turn out right because the legs and thighs will be done cooking long before the breasts. Unless you love that traditional magazine-cover presentation, break a bird into pieces and cook separately. One trick is to wrap whole birds (grouse, pheasants, quail, etc.) in aluminum foil along with a pat of butter and a splash of Italian dressing. Toss the package on the grill or directly onto glowing coals and turn once after ten minutes. Ten minutes later you'll have the most succulent, juiciest game bird you've ever eaten! If you like to cook low and slow, add plenty of liquid. Impress non-hunters and hunters alike by serving birds with a little apricot jam or cherry compote on top.

Open a Beer Bottle without an Opener, and Pour It the Right Way

Grasp the beer bottle's neck with your nondominant hand like a baseball bat, so only the cap shows above your grip. With your other hand, insert a spoon, cigarette lighter base, or other rigid tool (even the cap edge of another beer bottle) under the cap edge, using the base of your topmost (index) finger as a fulcrum. Carefully lever the cap off.

To pour, use a clean glass—ideally, chilled. Angle your glass at about forty-five degrees, and pour from the bottle (you are buying top shelf beer, right?) to hit the glass about an inch from the top. If there is little or no "head" (foam) once you've poured a half glass, turn the glass upright and pour directly into the center of the beer. With practice, you'll achieve the ideal: an inch or so of head. Now go out and get plenty of practice!

Stay Warm in Your Sleeping Bag

Buy a sleeping bag that is rated for the temperatures you expect to encounter. Wear dry sleeping apparel—the clothes you wore all day will be soaked with your perspiration and will slowly wick the heat from your body. Eat or drink something warm before bed (I prefer hot buttered rum). Wear warm socks and a stocking cap. Buy a sleeping bag that has enough room in the foot, shoulder and hip areas—body parts compressing against the bag guarantee an uncomfortable night's sleep.

Use a sleeping pad to insulate you from the cold ground or air circulating below your cot. Use a waterproof ground sheet (space blanket, etc.) as a vapor barrier under you or your tent to prevent bone-chilling moisture from seeping into your sleeping bag. If it gets extremely cold, wrap yourself in another vapor barrier (leave room for your head to ensure you can breathe!).

Driving on Muddy Roads

Go slow. Avoid braking as it will lock your wheels and you'll slide across the mud. Use a low gear and four-wheel drive. Look ahead on the road to anticipate a good line of travel and maintain your momentum. Move the steering wheel left to right as you negotiate ruts—the tire treads will grip the rut walls. Avoid exaggerated

Get more traction using the edges of your tire.

steering wheel movement and turns—the weight and momentum of your vehicle, not the tires, will carry the day on a slick surface.

If you get stuck, more weight on the drive wheels may generate additional traction. Put your friends in the truck bed over each wheel. Place branches, brush, floor mats, or small rocks in front of the drive tires to create some traction. "Rocking" back and forth by going from forward to reverse gears may get you out, but spinning the wheels at high speed simply digs you in deeper. Sometimes, all you need are a few inches of movement to get out of a rut—a small log, shovel handle, or other lever pushing on the bumper could be enough.

Toilet Paper Surrogates

Broad leaves (watch for poisonous plants), handfuls of grass, pages from a bad book, part of your topo map, receipts from your wallet. Snowballs, rounded stones, a bandanna, extra sock or shirt, the top of a sock, even a cap can work in an emergency. Simplify matters by carrying two or three prepackaged wet wipes in your pocket or pack.

Useful Knots Separate the Men from the Boys

You'll find a multitude of uses for a trucker's hitch, taut line hitch, bowline, square knot, and two half hitches. Rather than show you drawings, go to the following website and watch them being tied: www.animatedknots.com.

Find a Campsite

Proper campsite selection ensures physical safety and comfort. In all but the warmest weather, pitch your tent or park your trailer on a slight rise or knoll. Cool air sinks, so you won't be shivering all night. Hilltop breezes will keep mosquitoes at bay as well. On sweltering nights, do just the opposite.

In periods of cold weather pitch camp on a south-facing slope, which will catch the first warming rays of sun in the morning. If you expect rain, don't pitch your tent under big trees. The drips will drive you to distraction long after the shower ends. Wind could also knock loose a large branch—one reason they are called widowmakers. A copse of smaller trees will create shade and buffer strong winds.

Break Up a Dog Fight

Never grab dogs by the collar—you are not strong enough to keep two fighting dogs apart for very long and a fighting dog has no regard for even the best of owners. He could inadvertently bite you as you reach for him.

It takes two people to break up a dog fight. Each person will pick up the back legs of a dog and pull them in a backward-circular motion as if the dog were a wheelbarrow. This makes the dog sidestep with his front feet or fall, so he has little incentive or ability to bite you. Do not release the dogs—keep pulling them away from each other into separate rooms, yards, etc.

If you are alone, find a leash, loop it around the waist of one dog by threading the clip end through the hand loop. Pull that dog to a post, pole, or other secure object and tie the leash to it. A serious fight, of course, will continue. Next, grab the other dog by his back legs and circle as above, isolating it in another yard or room. Release the tied dog only when the other one is safely isolated in a secure location.

Delivering the Coup de Grâce to a Wounded Bird

Here's one method: Hold the bird (wings tight against the body) with your dominant hand. Face it away from the broad, flat portion of your gun stock or other hard object and swing his body with a snap to conk his head against the hard object.

Wringing a bird's neck quickly and cleanly is more difficult (and messy) than it appears. "Cervical dislocation" is much more humane: Grasp both of the bird's legs in your nondominant hand. Wrap your dominant index finger and thumb around the bird's neck just below the head, so the back of the bird's head is in the crook of the finger and thumb. As you stretch your dominant arm straight out you will put tension on the bird's body. When you reach the limit of stretching the bird bend the head back and increase tension so that the vertebrae is separated from the skull.

The "taxidermist's squeeze" is another method: Hold the bird by its breast, fingers, and thumb in its "armpits." Squeeze—hard—and hold until you've stopped both breathing and heartbeat.

Plant a Training Bird

There are a variety of ways to "dizzy" or "sleep" a training bird. This one works for me most of the time. Hold the bird in both hands and swing the body in short quick arcs (a few inches) so its head swings back and forth. Some prefer a circular motion—if you like that, use it. The key is getting the bird's head to swivel.

After ten to twenty seconds, tuck the bird's head under one wing, and then hold the head under the wing with one hand while holding the bird's feet with the other. Lay the bird on its side with the head down and tucked under it, and while continuing to hold it gently pull its legs straight back (away from the head). Hold legs and bird down for a second or two, and then sneak away.

Bootlaces That Stay Tied

Put the bow on the back of your boot. Lace as usual, but after the top eyelet, tie an overhand knot and then loop the laces around to the back of your leg.

Help Someone Find You

Most hunters can survive for hours or even days with basic survival skills when lost, but at some point wouldn't it be great if someone came looking for you? A survival plan will boost the chances you'll be found.

A friend and I once counted seven "Deer Creeks" we'd fished and five different "Grouse Mountains" in our hunting bailiwick. You can imagine how that might confuse someone searching for us. Besides telling someone where you're going, mark it on a map and leave a copy of the map with them.

Make a print of your boot soles. Searchers can get a head start using this telltale evidence. This goes double for kids in any outdoor setting. To make a print, simply place a sheet of aluminum foil on soft ground or carpet and step on it—with both boots.

I've made an informal study of search and rescue reports over the last few years. It's clear to me that just a few recurring errors are to blame for many of the volunteer callouts. Avoid them and you could save lives or at least the time, effort, and risk of the worthy volunteers who end up bailing you out.

Take a few minutes before each outing to charge your cell phone battery. Avoid bucking snowdrifts on a road—they only get worse the farther up the road you go. Take a map and compass course or teach yourself how to find a major road if you get lost. Bring water. Tell someone where you're going and when to expect you back. Carry a waterproof layer of clothing. Learn how to build a life-sustaining fire.

10

Tips from Guides, Outfitters, and Trainers

"Playing the game means treating your dogs like gentlemen, and your gentlemen like dogs."
—Ted Tally, *Terra Nova*

I AM GRATEFUL to everyone who has ever taken me hunting, including friends, club members, professional guides, dog trainers, outfitters, and lodge and preserve operators. From each I've heard fascinating stories, seen some incredible country, and gleaned bits and pieces of information that I now share with you.

Next time you are lucky enough to be invited hunting, savor the experience, not just for the birds in the bag but for the knowledge and insights you'll have gained. Acknowledge the provider appropriately with a quid pro quo, something in a bottle, or a heartfelt "Thank you."

Had I known I was going to write this book when I started jotting down these tips I could have thanked everyone personally. You know who you are, and please know that I appreciate your contributions to my, and now many others', hunting experiences. These tips have resulted in safer, more productive and enjoyable trips and training for me. I'm sure they'll work for you too.

- If your dog is licking all the medicine off a wound, put something tastier on another accessible part of his body.

- Use small bits of uncooked hot dog as your food reward when training a pup. Dogs swallow them after one quick chomp so they won't be distracted from your next command by their own noisy, crunchy chewing. They also emit a strong aroma, giving them long-distance reward value.

- Want another reason to approach a pointed bird wide of your dog? He won't be directly under the muzzle blast and its deafening effect. He'll also have one less excuse for not hearing your commands.

- When training a complex command, start with the last part and add the other parts in reverse order. When you get to the beginning, it will be a downhill ride.

- As the day goes on and the ground heats up, warm air rises from the bottom of draws, valleys, and river canyons, creating an uphill or upstream breeze almost everywhere. As the sun rises, hunt from above the best bird hideouts and you'll help your dog intercept scent as he leads you along a ridgeline or down a draw.

- Sports shows—especially on the last day—can be a bargain-hunter's paradise, whether you're shopping for gear or a guided trip.

- You might have better luck getting a lost dog returned to you if you change the information on his collar tag. Leave his name off—fewer thieves are interested in stealing a dog whose name they don't know because he will be less likely to respond to their commands. Avoid engraving "Reward" and then your phone numbers on the tag. It could encourage ransom requests. Instead, put "Requires daily medication" on the tag. Good-hearted folk will work hard to return your dog, and bad apples will avoid a dog that might cost them money.

- Do you own a Tri-Tronics Upland G3 Special? Turning on the beeper remotely from the collar is sometimes difficult. Try this: Once you've pressed the button on the beeper to turn it on, hold the collar so the prongs on the battery unit face the base of the beeper. Then hit the green button on the handheld transmitter to turn it on or off.

- Chukar hunters should be loath to give up altitude. If you are finding birds at one elevation, stay there, side-hilling to cover ground. Unless there's a good reason, don't follow escaping birds downhill only to have to climb back up again.

- The best bedding in an outside dog kennel or house is grass hay. It breaks down slower than straw and makes minimal dust. Cedar shavings are strong smelling and might impact a dog's scenting ability.

- Remove the entrails of shot birds immediately after they're retrieved to help them cool quickly. In wintry conditions, stuff some snow into the body cavity. Scuff a hole in the dirt and bury the guts—unless your dog is riding in the back of the truck—bird innards are excellent fart fuel.

Fogless shooting glasses.

- When fogged-over shooting glasses leave you stranded in a pea soup of your own making, turn your hat around. Put the bill in back where it won't catch your exhaled breath, hang around your glasses, and condense on the lens.

- Introduce all current and new dogs to each other on neutral territory. When picking up new puppies we meet in the breeder's yard, not mine, and avoid turf battles. The same strategy works with dogs that are going to hunt together.

- Having trouble getting your dog to give up whatever he's got in his mouth? Gently pinch the loose skin on his flank, or blow sharply right into his nose. If that won't work, toss your hat or something else into his line of sight. He may chase after it, dropping the bird.

- Lost your dog? Track into the wind, as there's a good chance he got a whiff of something attractive like a deer, possum, or female dog. Notify mail carriers, etc. Put a shirt you've worn, along with a bowl of water, where you last saw him and check back in the morning.

- Burning eyes and fatigue are common early signs of dehydration in humans. Drink plenty of water while hunting or training.

- As you approach a bird to flush it, don't focus on where the bird is sitting—look in the general direction you expect it to fly. Your eyes (let alone your gun muzzle) can't move as fast as a flushing bird and you'll likely shoot behind it.

- If yours is an "outside dog," in winter you can boost the fat content of his diet to keep him warm. Some veterinarians recommend a couple of tablespoons of olive oil on dry food, while others suggest butter or coconut oil.

- A warm room is all the heat soggy leather boots can tolerate. Avoid setting them near a heater, floor register, or fireplace. Stuff them with newspaper to wick some of the interior moisture away. An alternative is to use a commercial boot dryer.

- Having trouble opening that barbed-wire gate? Can't get the post into the wire loop? Before you pull the gate toward the post that's anchored in the ground, stretch the top strand of the gate wire by pulling from the middle to stretch it. If that doesn't help, make sure you've put the bottom of the post as far as possible into the wire loop located at ground level. If you're lucky enough to find a short pole anchored by a length of wire to the nearby post you're trying to reach, loop it through the gate and apply some leverage.

- If you use a bota or squirt bottle to give your dog water, aim for the side of their mouth near the corner. More water actually gets into his belly that way, rather than dripping out. A straight-down-the-throat shot might cause him to cough.

- All the modern electronic gizmos we take outdoors these days are worthless without instructions, so pack them in your kit as well. Don't forget a spare pair of reading glasses (equally useful when doctoring dogs).

Aim for the side of his mouth for less waste, no coughing.

- If you can, approach chukars from above—start your hunt at the top of a hill and only go downhill enough to find them. Bonus: you'll have cut off their usual escape route—uphill.
- Use as low a volume to deliver your voice commands as will work in your situation. A dog's hearing is much better than ours and may construe increased volume as a show of anger.
- If you carry a Space Blanket in your survival kit, check it every year for age-related rips. I opened mine once and found that every fold had become a full-length tear. Luckily, I made the discovery at home, not in the woods on a cold, rainy night.
- Light your camp lantern before dark. You may have a hard time finding it after the sun sets.
- Permethrin is the most effective tick spray if you use it right. That means applying it to your clothing before you venture out. Hang, spray, and let dry for at least two hours before you head out. In formulations for clothing, permethrin is not appropriate for dogs.
- One of the best fire starters is a tangerine-sized ball of duct tape.
- Warm up by fueling your internal furnace. Carbohydrates burn fastest, proteins slowest. Best is a snack food that offers both for sustained energy.
- Buy a bandanna. Silk or rayon, get the big ones that real buckaroos wear, available at farm supply and western stores. Keeps your neck—and the rest of your body, in turn—warm. Bandannas are good for a multitude of other uses around camp from sweatbands to oven mitts.
- Gates are designed to keep livestock in or out. Leave open gates open, closed gates closed.
- For quick energy, change your socks in the middle of the day. Your feet sweat eight ounces of moisture a day. Fresh, dry socks mean a happier hunter.
- Move cows off a road with slow, gradual "body language." Don't get too close, but walk toward them slowly, arms outstretched, scarecrow style, moving in the direction you want them to go. There is a sweet spot—not too close—that will push cattle without splitting the herd. Yelling, running, or waving your hat will induce panic and a potential stampede—usually in the wrong direction. With several hunters, set up a picket line all moving together. If you're driving and want to split a herd to get through, be mindful that calves will blindly follow their mothers, so go slow and use your peripheral vision to avoid panicking those surprisingly nimble youngsters.

11

Your Questions, My Answers

"Man is a dog's idea of what God should be."

—Holbrook Jackson

I WISH I COULD hunt with all of you. The camaraderie, insights from dogs and owners, and the give-and-take that occur during a walk in the field are invaluable. I can't bring you along on our TV shoots, so I've asked viewers to correspond via Facebook, blog, and my "Take Your Kid Hunting" surveys. The questions you've asked are fascinating and thought provoking. Here are some of the most common and interesting ones. Keep them coming at www.facebook.com/wingshootingusa.

Q: Does hunting a younger dog and older dog together help the younger dog learn quicker?

A: Yes. But he learns both the good habits and the bad. A young dog needs to become bold and confident, and that won't happen if he's following, chasing, imitating, or playing grab-ass with an older dog.

Q: How soon do you introduce your dogs to the "Heel" command?

A: If your dog can walk and knows his name, you can introduce the concept of "Heel," but do it gently. I like Rick and Ronnie Smith's technique with their "Wonder Lead." And remember, young dogs are like flies—sugar works better than vinegar if you want results. A couple of well-done "Heels" are plenty for a pup, especially when you focus on praise rather than correction.

Q: Have you ever encountered a dog that just couldn't be trained to hunt?

A: I've owned them. Just kidding; but there probably are dogs that are less inclined to hunt. Much of that can be blamed on genetics and bad owners who haven't trained their dog to basic obedience. I might guess that any dog with three or more legs (not joking) and a nose can hunt . . . if motivated by birds and their human.

Cattle tanks are a great water source in desert country.

Q: I hunt a lot of grouse and ducks in Minnesota and I have springer spaniels. When hunting them in the woods they don't like to get off the trail. What can I do to help them understand to go into the woods?

A: How much contact have they had with live birds? If you're not finding a lot of birds in the woods, set up some training situations where they will discover birds when they get off trail. Once they get the idea, they'll be more inclined to venture out.

Q: To neuter or not to neuter? I'm in the process of purchasing my first bird dog and have been given a lot of advice on what to do and what not to do when getting your first bird dog. On several occasions I have heard discussions about whether or not to get your dog fixed or neutered. Some say that if you do get your dog fixed, they will not be able to hunt longer and will be less aggressive in the field. Is this true?

A: Having just lived through our most recent neutering, I haven't seen any change in Manny's field behavior. The problems you worry about are easily fixed with good conditioning and training. The simple answer is, if you aren't going to breed or show your dog, neutering will prevent unwanted pregnancies and possibly dampen the roaming instinct in males seeking females in heat. The research on whether neutered males are more prone to certain cancers is not conclusive. Certainly they aren't vulnerable to testicular cancer! Many old wives will suggest a neutered dog is less aggressive, but there is little clinical evidence to support that. Most research indicates postponing neutering for at least eighteen months or more to ensure that the dog's body develops fully and receives all the benefits of the hormones generated from the testes.

Q: Scott, you mentioned placing tape on your shooting glasses so that you use your right eye. I was checking that out and noticed I close my left eye. I really never noticed it before. What are the pros and cons to closing an eye while shooting?

A: If you shoot better with your left eye closed, you might be cross dominant like me. The tape ensures that I don't have to remember to close my eye—instead, it muddles my left-dominant eye's vision enough so my right takes over (I shoot righty).

Q: What's the longest distance you like to have your dog hunt in front of you and still be shotgun range?

A: Presuming that you're talking about flushing breeds, "gun range" should be the distance from you that puts birds in the air within a range you can ethically shoot at them. A dog should probably work ten to fifteen yards in front of you so you have another twenty to thirty yards of viable range after a bird is flushed. Pointing breeds range according to genetics and training, but "gun range" is less an issue because (theoretically) they hold their birds until you get there.

Q: My question pertains to retriever training. Many if not most professionals encourage developing a personal bond between the owner and dog before moving on to advanced training. One such technique is the simple game of "fetch" to establish rapport and basic commands that can be built upon. My question concerns my wonderfully eager and cooperative English cocker who is so eager to please that she is almost nonstop at retrieving. I ordered your new Signature Series dummy for variety as well as to teach familiarity with an attached wing. My dog is still of the puppy mindset at eighteen months, easily wearing out my throwing arm before herself. She was a started puppy at seven months when I acquired her, eagerly retrieving flapping pigeons nearly her own size. Is it possible to overdo the dummy business such that she will lose interest in, or forget, about the real thing? An experienced dog trainer friend has cautioned me against this. My dog loves to play so much that I would hate to deny her the fun, especially since she does it to eagerly please me.

A: Sounds like you're having a great time. Yep, the bonding thing is important. I would agree with the trainer (which I am not) that you could burn out your pup. At some point, retrieving must become a command, obeyed every time in every situation (force training). I face the same situation, though, with my two-and-a-half-year-old wirehair. So, I divorce the two: There is play time with a tennis ball and no retrieving-related commands. And then, out comes the Real Bird Bumper or real birds, and "Fetch."

Q: I notice in the magazines, big trials, and even hunt tests that many dogs have long names. And sometimes they have unusual spellings of common names! What gives?

A: You can thank the American Kennel Club and other breed registries. Every registered dog requires a distinct name for record-keeping purposes, so many owners have become quite creative. Add to that limits on the number of characters on the registration form, plus many breeders who require you to preface your dog's name with their kennel name, and it can get pretty complicated.

Q: I have an English setter. I got him at one and a half years old. How would you start training him? He was quite shy when I got him but he is coming out of that. And he does come when called. I have taken him in the woods where I know there are plenty of grouse and he shows interest. I do keep him on a long lead at this time. Did I do right?

A: Sounds like you're already training if he comes when called. He also seems to be bonding to you and trusting you. Continue your obedience training and start the gun dog work now, in your yard. A long lead he can drag along until he's solid on his "Come" command is always a good idea. You could have started the hunting training sooner, but with the foundation you've laid, I'll bet you two will do just fine.

Q: What's the best way to teach a young dog to honor another dog's point?

A: Honoring or backing is really an obedience issue, not a natural pointing skill. Like any other aspect of "Whoa," your dog needs to learn that the sight of another dog on point is a visual command to "Whoa." That's the easy part. The hard part is the practice to perfection.

Q: Which problem is the easier fix, a shoe brusher or a dog that hunts too wide?

A: Sometimes it's not that simple. I like both strategies at times. In heavy cover or a field crowded with birds, you'd want a dog that works close. In sparse country with spread-out birds, you'd want a big runner. Many well-bred versatile dogs will adjust their range to the conditions. I'm no pro trainer, but many spaniel guys think you can adjust a dog's range somewhat (barring genetics) by frequently planting training birds at the distance you want a dog to range. I don't know that harsher "solutions" such as electronic collars when he ranges too far will work and may in fact diminish a dog's enthusiasm for birds in general.

Q: Do you prefer to allow your pointing hunting dog to stay steady to shot and flush, or just flush?

A: If you have watched my show, you know my dogs are seldom steady to wing, shot, and fall. Wing-clipped birds due to my bad shooting deserve a dog that is off at the shot to catch those injured runners. I'm working on getting Manny steady, though, because of the risk of someone shooting a low bird over a chasing dog. I'm also leery of the cliffs and other topographical hazards where we hunt that a dog might not see as he chases. I'd rather have the option of releasing a steady dog than trying to "Whoa" a running dog once he takes off after the shot.

Q: My dog begins to hunt closer to me the more I shoot, until he is walking next to me. He shows no signs of being gun shy for the first two or three birds. Is there something I can do to help him stay focused?

A: I wonder if it's gun shyness. If so, you might consider starting over to introduce the gun appropriately. But also look at what happens during and after the shot: Are you shooting over him (which could be painful or deafening)? Is he

Typical chukar country: cheatgrass,
rimrock, and elevation changes.

being pecked or clawed by a live bird on a retrieve? What are you saying or doing after the shot? Do you praise him for a solid retrieve? Revisit each incident and find the common thread. Most bird dogs are enthusiastic hunters, and when they are not there is a good reason for it.

Q: I have a five-year-old British Labrador and would like to know more about the best type of food to feed him. I am not sure I understand the difference or true benefit of grain free versus food with grain in it, especially as a dog matures and ages. Also, most brands offer canned wet food as well as their dry brands. What is your opinion on alternating or including canned wet foods in my dog's daily diet?

A: Most premium-priced foods are just fine for most hunting dogs. I'm no nutritionist but would suggest active dogs need more calories and "energy," which generally comes from protein and fat (as opposed to carbohydrates for humans). The grain question becomes more of an issue as a dog ages because grain-free foods are often very high in protein and fat and a retired or lethargic dog can bulk up quickly. For me, dry food works best when traveling (no cans or openers). I add water to every dog's food every feeding to ensure adequate hydration. If a dog won't eat after a hunt, wet food or other incentives help but they are expensive on a per-pound basis. As long as the food package states that your choice is a "complete" diet, you'll be fine. Ask your veterinarian for specific advice about your dog based on how, where, and when you hunt and how much real energy your dog is likely to expend on a daily basis.

Q: Do certain breeds adapt better to being house dogs as opposed to outside kennels?

A: Despite stereotypes, I've seen all types of hunting dogs function well while living as a part of the family in the home. It's more about breeding, training (human and canine), and how your family is configured.

Q: I'm new to bird hunting. I currently have a six-year-old old German wirehair that I've had about six months. He's a good dog but the problem is he fights with other male dogs. To try to correct this, the man I got him from had him neutered but this didn't seem to help. Is this common in the breed?

A: It doesn't have to be. You should start over. Consider this dog a pup and re-socialize him to people, dogs, cats, horses . . . even Democrats. Additionally, talk with an obedience trainer or behaviorist about socializing a dog. Neutering is not the panacea many think it is.

Q: I currently own a Lab and she's been great but I'm considering a Brittany or other upland bird dog breed that we can use for bird hunting and home life with me, my wife, and three daughters.

A: Your Lab should do fine in the uplands so save yourself time and money unless you really want a pointing dog. Just train the retriever to stay within gun range. The five of you can't possible wear out a Labrador retriever!

Q: What is the best way to train a dog to work a blood trail for deer?

A: Same way the violinist got to Carnegie Hall: practice! Waken a dog's nose to tracking by salting your yard with hot dog bits. Add a command word or phrase ("Find 'em!") and soon he'll understand that he should put the nose down and start working the trail. Start with slow and deliberate work on a check cord, and then begin training on short, straight line tracks, reminding the dog often of his job and praising him every time he does it right.

Q: How do you keep your dog from becoming distracted on the hunt?

A: Show them more birds. Does your dog know that the be-all and end-all in hunting is birds in his mouth? If he gets enough positive feedback for his efforts (dead birds) he'll glom onto it and begin ignoring deer, butterflies, other hunters, etc.

Q: I have a black Lab that is going on age four this year. She is a wonderful dog but when I throw the training dummy she will pick it up, go about ten steps, and drop it. When I try to correct her she acts like her world just came to an end. How can I get her to follow through with a retrieve?

A: Force training is the sure way. Short term, I would rethink your "correction." Does she know what you're asking her to do from start to finish? For a possible temporary fix, you can run away from her as she begins her retrieve and she might chase you. Slow or stop when she catches up, and poof! She's there, by you, with the dummy. As an alternative training method, keep a check cord on her and simply reel her in.

Q: My Brittany is very hardheaded and will not respond to commands when we first arrive in the field. He eventually responds as he tires. Is there anything you can recommend that will make him respond when first in the field?

A: Your dog is simply learning that he can disobey your commands. It all starts with yard work. If a dog doesn't obey your commands, every time, in your backyard, he certainly won't in the field. Make the transition from yard to field a gradual one. Begin just outside your yard at first, move farther away, etc. Keep a check cord on your dog at all times and don't give a command unless you can immediately enforce it. Transition to an electronic collar if necessary.

Q: My son is looking to buy a dog to go pheasant hunting. We are considering a German shorthaired pointer. Any suggestions you would have would be great!

A: Get a flushing breed. Most pheasants run most often and a pointing breed will be much harder to train to carefully track and stay on point when birds are running.

Q: Do all Labs train and hunt the same no matter yellow, black, or chocolate? If not, is there a better choice to pick to train a Lab pointer for upland hunting?

A: In my experience, a dog can wear polka dots and still hunt well. It's about breeding and training. Research the breeder and line carefully, get lots of references, and watch the pup's parents work in the field if possible. A little history: For some time brown Labs were thought to be a mutation or even evidence of an outcross. Genetic testing squashed that old wives' tale.

Q: What do you think about rescue dogs?

A: There are many rescue dogs that are well trained, socialized, and eager to hunt again. I'd venture to say most dogs that end up in rescue were put there for the best of reasons: they deserve another chance or they had an owner who could no longer hunt. Rescued dogs seem to know you've saved their lives and they will love you forever.

Q: How do you prepare hunting dogs for the upcoming season as far as food and conditioning? Do you start putting them on

a high-performance food and, if so, how far in advance? I have found that walking or running them in the fields does not condition them enough for hunting, so what are the alternatives?

A: I feed high-protein, high-fat food year-round because my dogs get a lot of exercise. Buddy's feed is about thirty-three percent protein and twenty percent fat. Any higher ratio and he gets fat. Manny gets thirty-eight to forty percent protein and thirty percent fat and I still can't bulk him up. If you choose to feed a maintenance diet in the off-season, experts suggest feeding the performance ration at least sixty days prior to the season. That way your dog's system has time to metabolize the higher levels of nutrients and turn them into muscle and energy.

As far as conditioning, most pro trainers use some sort of "roading." Simply put, roading involves a dog pulling, or pulling against, some type of weight (chain, sled, ATV) to build muscles in a different way than free running. If nothing else, longer runs alongside your bike or even free running are better than nothing for both of you!

Q: After hunting a few generations of setters and training them all different ways, I have found that the best technique is to get into the field as much as possible. Most dogs know how to hunt and teach me better than I am able to teach them. Do you find this to be true? Additionally do you find that starting a dog as a puppy, or waiting until they are two years old or so, works best?

A: We learn as much from our dogs as they learn from us. Sure, they learn by running around in a field, but some of what they learn is not what we want in a finished dog. We can help them become better hunters with careful guidance, along with plenty of bird contacts and field time. On your other question, dogs learn by watching us from the day we bring them home. Knowing that, why not jump-start

This is a "chain gang" of more Weimaraners than you'll usually see at a field trial.

their training? Just set your expectations at an appropriate level and you'll probably get an extra season from your young companion simply because you started him sooner.

Q: How does one locate guides with dogs that hunt public land in the West? The five-star experience is not necessary for many of us.

A: There are very few public-land upland guides out West. Try the Internet and ask for a lot of references if you find any. Join groups like Pheasants Forever and the Ruffed Grouse Society and ask them for members who guide. Local chambers of commerce in hunting hotspots like South Dakota can also help. Subscribe to the bird-hunting magazines and look at the ads for more options.

Q: For someone who is starting out using dogs, what can we expect to go wrong?

A: Got a week? Just kidding. You will have days when everything seems to go wrong. When this happens, just pick up the pieces and learn from them. Don't hold a grudge. Not accounting for the puppy-related issues like housebreaking, you'll need to cope with dominance (you must be the pack boss using psychology, not force); obedience (never give a command you can't immediately enforce); and, for pointing breeds, steadiness when standing birds.

Q: My son would like a hunting dog. What breed would you recommend for a first timer?

A: Flushing breeds require a few less commands than pointers before they are ready to hunt. You don't have to teach steadiness while pointing, for one thing.

Q: I own a ten-year-old Lab. She is in pretty good shape. What should I be concerned about when considering hunting her for birds this fall?

A: Hunt as long as she's willing. Keep a close eye on her, watch for dehydration, note when she acts tired, and beware of heat issues. If she shows signs of soreness at night, it may be time for Rimadyl or another anti-inflammatory.

Q: I have a three-year-old Lab that loves life. My problem with her is that I cannot calm her down in the field or other unfamiliar situations

until she burns herself out. Do you have any tips on how I can work on this with her?

A: I wonder if this is an obedience issue? Practicing "Sit" or "Whoa" when she meets people or the doorbell rings might help. It might be as simple as gradually exposing her to more unfamiliar situations, from shopping to walking on the sidewalk. In the field, a high-strung dog should still obey your commands, so go back to the yard or house and start over, expecting total conformity to your commands. Try a few warm-up drills involving obedience commands before you turn her loose in the field to remind her she's working. I still put my young dog through some obedience drills before and during a hunt.

Q: Why are heavier loads needed for wild birds as opposed to club birds?

A: Wild birds often flush farther from the gun and fly faster, so shots are usually at longer distances.

Q: I see you have a German wirehaired pointer. I am interested in getting a pointer. My question is several of my friends have flushing breeds. What kind of problems can a person run into hunting these different breeds together?

A: This kind of mix usually doesn't work well. A pointer will quickly get jealous of a flusher crashing into the birds he's standing. He'll start breaking point, fights will take place, prom dates will be broken, etc. Hunt very far apart (say 300 or more yards) and it may work.

Q: Both my wife and I are gun enthusiasts but have never hunted birds. We are both in the autumn of our years and would like to get a bird dog. Where do we start?

A: What a great way to spend your retirement! A dog is a lifelong commitment, so before you make the emotional and financial investment be sure you really want to invest the training time and effort into a dog and will truly spend enough time in the field with it. Hunt at a preserve a few times with their guides and dogs, find a club, and help out at training days. Attend some hunt tests and club events. "Borrow" a well-behaved dog for a day and night or two to see if a dog will fit into your lifestyle. If you're still high on a dog and hunting, you've already done much of the research for a dog that might fit your hunt style, locale, birds you'll be hunting, and personality.

Q: What are the advantages and disadvantages of getting a started dog versus a puppy and which would you recommend for someone new to or returning to the sport of bird hunting?

A: I'm bullish on buying started dogs. I've always gotten pups, but that's just my preference. A started dog means no midnight potty runs and obedience classes. And the started, adopted, and rescued dogs that I know have bonded just fine with their new humans. Puppies are magical beings, and the experience of raising one is special, but it's not for everyone.

Q: I have a seven-month-old field bred springer. She is very high octane and has a hard time listening until she has had some exercise. Is there anything I can do other than keep working with her and letting her mature?

A: Nope.

Q: Is it necessary for a dog to have a beard, wire hair, and a docked tail in order to be a good hunting dog? I have noticed from watching your show with your dogs, Buddy and six-month-old Manny, that you prefer German wirehaired pointers. I live in South Carolina and my son and I utilize our "official" state dog, the Boykin spaniel, but these dogs often have health issues. I was wondering why you prefer the wirehair breed? And do they have any unusual health issues like Boykins, such as ear problems and thyroid issues?

A: Those physical attributes do have function, but for me they're just a personal preference. All well-bred hunting dogs will deliver in the field and at home, so find a breed and breeder you like and go for it! Some wirehaired breeds may have ectopic or entropic eyelids, but it's not much of a worry. Most breeds have health issues unique to them, so do your research.

Q: Which western state would you consider the best for multiple types of upland bird hunting?

A: That's like asking me which of my dogs I like most! Every state has terrain, bird species, and scenery that make it unique. Some that fit your request include Montana (Huns, sage grouse, sharptails, pheasants, forest grouse), the Dakotas (all of the above plus prairie chickens). All three of those have great public access programs too.

Q: My dog has had his rattlesnake shots. However, I've heard that you should also give your dog antihistamine if your dog is bitten. Is this true and how does it help?

A: Antihistamine will reduce tissue swelling. A snake-bit dog risks windpipe swelling to the point it closes off, suffocating him. And remember that vaccine works for some, but not all, varieties of rattlers.

Q: What kind of training can I use to keep my shorthair on point after the bird flushes?

A: Start in the yard, on a training table if you have one. Introduce handheld birds from a distance with your dog on a check cord and half-hitch on the flank. Eventually, you can bring them closer to your dog, and then start again far away with someone throwing birds, or use a launcher while you relax your dog and command "Whoa." Bring the flushes closer, train in multiple locations, start introducing gunfire, and when you finally get to a hunting situation, keep a check cord on your dog. Let someone else do the shooting while you handle your dog. Many pro trainers "proof" their dog with massive exposure to birds while the dog obeys the "Whoa" command. They'll have birds flapping in his face, walking around, thrown nearby, etc. I like this technique more and more these days.

Q: How do you tell a prairie chicken from a hen pheasant?

A: Hens have much longer tails and in flight that might be the best distinction. In hand, chicken breast feathers have a horizontal barring pattern. Chickens are also more black-and-white than brown-and-white, like hens or sharptails, but I'm color blind, so I have trouble when birds are silhouetted in the air. For this reason I pass on a lot of shots.

Q: I'm looking into getting my first hunting dog. I would like one to take pheasant hunting as well as duck and goose hunting. I live in Iowa, where it gets very cold in the winter and he'll be going into the icy water after some birds. What is an ideal breed for my situation?

A: Labrador retriever.

Q: My dog's only (Ha-Ha!) fault is a serious case of lockjaw. Doesn't eat or chew the bird, just doesn't want to let go. Any suggestions?

A: Force fetch! This is an obedience issue. Short term, blow in his nose or pinch his flank and he might give up the bird. With a pup, you can toss your hat on the ground and he may drop the bird to chase it.

Q: What if your host's dog continues to bring your downed birds to you? Do you take the bird(s), or wait for the owner to retrieve your bird?

A: Most dogs will fetch all downed birds to their handler, but when this happens, ask the owner what he wants the dog to do. If he wants the dog to bring birds only to him, turn your back on the dog as he retrieves.

Q: My older dog has always been a big runner and covers lots of ground, but I have questioned his stamina. I really noticed it with my younger dog. I generally hunt them in thirty- to forty-five-minute sessions and then have them come in for water. I carry water while hunting just in case they would like a drink. By the third round the older dog is a foot polisher. Any conditioning tips?

A: We can't walk enough to get our dogs in shape for all-day hunts, even if we rotate dogs. Work up to long bike rides (eight to fifteen miles) a couple of times per week. Periodically "roading" your dogs (having them pull against a sled or ATV rigged for the purpose) builds different muscles. Long term, a high-protein, high-fat diet fed year-round will also help. A high-fat supplement during the hunt might help. I like Vita-Cal but anything with a lot of fat and little volume that he'll eat might help.

Q: What is the best way to desensitize your dog to gunfire? Is there any way to cure a gun-shy dog?

A: Long, slow, gradual exposure to noise, from a distance

The original version of "roading," a dog in harness trotting ahead of the horse.

at first and always associated with the fun of birds—chasing and retrieving—should work on a young dog that is not already gun shy. Consult a training pro if your dog is steadfastly gun shy.

Q: I have a Brittany male, two years old. We hunt preserves here in Delaware. I use an electronic collar, whistle, and beeper for training and when we are in the field. Lately he has started straying away from me. How can I correct this? I keep this little dog with me most of the time, in the house, out for walks on a leash, etc. He is my retirement buddy.

A: Lucky you. A Britt sure beats TV and crotchety poker buddies! Running big is not the issue some think it is as long as he will come when called or whistled. If he's not stone-cold broke to "Come," work on that in the yard and then in the field under various conditions and at several locations. Use the electronic collar correctly but only when needed. Train him to be staunch once he points (no matter the distance), and the only problem becomes your getting to him and the bird in time for a shot. In most cases, a dog's range is a dog's range, inherited to a great degree. Trying to change that may lead to other obedience issues.

Q: Why is it that English setters squat very low to the ground when they point in Europe, as opposed to in American style, where they stand with their tail up?

A: "Setting" was what these dogs did in the early days before guns. Hunters used nets to capture birds, and a dog that laid down after pointing would not obstruct the net when the hunter threw it. Europeans are funny these ways, and often ignore the style many American field trialers and magazine editors want in pointing breeds.

Q: What is your opinion on using a fishing pole and bird wing on a young pup? Is it just a way to see instincts early or, as some suggest, a way to steady the pup on point and adjust his position?

A: Fishing is fun, but really doesn't prove anything because sight pointing is not what a bird dog will ultimately be required to do. I don't know that it even "proves" any real instinct.

Q: When should a puppy begin training on upland birds?

A: When you're ready to begin. Keep your expectations at an appropriate level for the pup, but why not acquaint them with birds and the fun associated with them, at twelve weeks? He may not hold a point, certainly won't reliably retrieve, but make it fun as you introduce him to feathers.

Q: What's the best way to teach a Chesapeake to hunt upland birds?

A: Take him out and try it. If he quarters the field and hunts within gun range, comes when called, and retrieves, you're done.

Q: It's been said that hunting dogs should be kept in an outside kennel, not in the house, because it may harm their sense of smell and diminish their desire to hunt. What are your thoughts on this?

A: Poor field performance is more a matter of training than living conditions. My dogs smell great! They found ten birds yesterday, and they live in the house—actually are in the office with me right now. They learn their lessons faster and more completely when they are with me a lot. Dogs will work hardest for a human they like and respect, and that comes with regular interaction.

Q: We have a nine-year-old yellow Lab that is starting to lose her vision. Do you have any suggestions?

A: We all get there. Never forget how hard your dog worked for you when she could see well. Give her a good home until she goes to the great duck marsh in the sky. If you want to hunt her, you'll have to be very attentive. Maybe you can walk her at heel until retrieving time and give her that thrill in safe, controlled situations while a younger dog does the dirty work.

Q: What's the best way to teach your son to hunt?

A: Consider him just another pup. Take him along and let him watch your dog work. Hunt in small doses (a morning, an afternoon, rather than all day). He'll be hooked. When he shows serious interest, have him attend a hunter education course and introduce him to some easy clay target shooting.

Q: When training my German wirehaired pointer, I struggle to get him to range out farther than fifty to sixty yards. When we are in the grouse woods (where I do about ninety percent of my hunting) he is perfect, but I want him out farther when I make it to the Dakotas for pheasant. Any suggestions?

A: A wise trainer once told me a dog will range farther because there are no birds closer in. So, when you hit the wide-open prairies, your wirehair may naturally start extending his range. Many versatile dogs adjust range to the cover—sparser cover equals bigger pattern. If not, you can probably train your dog to reach out by planting training birds farther away than his normal range. Each dog has a natural range, but the chance to find birds will trump almost any other instinct.

Q: What has been your best method to "Whoa"-train your puppy?

A: Simply put, gradually introducing more—and more tempting—distractions (birds). A check cord is the go-to tool in my kennel as the physical restraint is helpful. Better still is a check cord that encircles the dog's waist and then goes through his back legs to a post. Any dog movement lifts at least a couple of legs off the ground, which is a very uncomfortable position for the dog that he will quickly learn to avoid. One reminder: "whoa" is an obedience command and is only distantly related to the pointing instinct upon scenting a bird.

Q: In your opinion, what's the number-one thing as far as obedience that you can teach a new gun dog?

A: I had my own opinion on this, but went to my friends for their ideas and it was, hands-down, "Here." Stopping a dog with "Whoa" is good, but what if he stops right where the trouble is? Your recall command brings him back to you, which is a good thing every time, unless he's being chased by a grizzly (true story!).

Q: I am just starting with my vizsla. We completed the Junior Hunter test and are now training for the Senior Hunter test. My question is, how can I best teach a solid "honor" if I don't train with other dogs?

A: At some point, you'll need several other dogs because practicing with the plywood imitations doesn't create the psychological temptation that a real dog offers. If you've joined a club, ask fellow members to help you (and vice versa). Their dog gets steadiness training, yours gets backing work. And remember, backing is an obedience skill triggered by the sight of a dog on point. Even a family pet will do in a pinch—all the "pointing" dog has to do is stand still so your trainee can come around the corner, see the point, and then honor.

Q: I have a four-year-old English pointer. When I give the "Whoa" command she stops but wilts. How can I get her to "Whoa" with style?

A: Why bother? You might be able to get your dog to hold her tail higher, but "Whoa" is an obedience command, not the visible manifestation of an instinctive scent-point-pounce sequence. If your dog is more intense on a real point (scenting a bird), count your blessings. You might also lighten up on how you deliver the "Whoa" command—be more encouraging and upbeat.

Q: My German shorthair pointer is a great hunting dog and companion for me and the whole family. Both her brother and sister belong to relatives. They will jump off a dock into a lake without hesitation but mine will only get into water if she can walk in and then only if her sister, brother, my kids, or I are already in the lake. Do you know of a way to increase her boldness around water?

A: Versatile dogs often have an aversion to water but need to be willing to search for downed birds in the drink. A good incentive is a bird. Live, wing-clipped ducks will lead a merry chase, and even dead birds are often enough motivation to get a shorthair into the water. Swinging a bird that's tethered to a line and pole

Hungarian partridge country. They could be anywhere.

out over water, tempting your laid-back non-swimmer into the water, can be a good start. Are you praising her water entry? Some trainers use the "Cheetos trick," floating those crispy treats in deeper and deeper water. All these tricks help in the early stages. Whether you'll ever entice her to get airborne, dock-dog style, shouldn't be a concern if you simply want a solid, working hunter.

Q: Dog breeders in Europe do not remove the dew claws from puppies. However, all the dog breeders I know in America remove them. Why the difference from Europe to America?

A: They've got a different set of values regarding animal rights in much of Europe. No tail-docking but mandatory neutering (talk about dichotomy), no tie-out stakes, etc. My guess is it's one more shortsighted case of nanny-stating the welfare of a dog without considering its ultimate use or lifestyle. Ironically, dewclaws rip and tear, causing pain for a lifetime, versus the few moments required for removal as a pup.

Q: What steps do you take to ensure your four-legged hunting buddy is taking on enough water? What signs do you watch for in regard to dehydration?

A: I carry water we can both drink in bota-style containers so I can squirt it into any mouth, canine or human. I offer water every few minutes when my dogs check in with me. It's easier to watch for a hot dog than a dehydrated dog, but pinching up a fold of skin between your dog's shoulders and watching how quickly it lies down again is one indication. An overheated dog won't stop panting even when rested; it also might search for shade or dig shallow holes to lie in. When this happens it's long past time to cool him down with water, internally and externally.

Q: My dog will not staunch up on wild birds even though I have him steady to wing and shot on pen-raised birds. I think it is due to shooting too many grouse over him his first year, birds that were not pointed. In fact, some were actually bumped by him. My last setter was so easy I thought it would be impossible to get a setter that wasn't all point-wrong. How do I recover?

A: Some might suggest more wild birds so eventually he'll learn he can't catch them. You can also train stop-to-flush with a check cord and pigeons or pen-raised birds. Once a dog scents birds and points, you can turn the situation into an obedience drill with a "Whoa." Pen raised or wild, single or covey, once he learns "Whoa," he needs to know he'd better not move or else. Finally, don't let him think that flushing birds equals chasing birds. Go slow and don't allow any variance from steadiness in the yard. The first several dozen flushes should be from quite a distance (fifteen to twenty-five yards).

Q: What's the biggest mistake owners make with hunting dogs in the field?

A: Forgetting to praise a dog that does his job well. Yard work is full of positive reinforcement, but we often toss all that away when we drop the tailgate and go hunting. Your dog still needs rewards if you want him to work hard for you.

Q: What's the best way to feed a dog pieces of wild game?

A: Why bother? Some handlers reward a good retrieve with the bird's head, but that could encourage eating the whole bird. Bones can lodge in throats or intestines. Many states require transported game to have heads intact. Giving a dog bird guts often results in rather odiferous payback. On the other hand, a bite-sized piece of venison backstsrap is always a welcome treat for a hardworking dog.

Q: It's so hard to train my Lab puppy. Any suggestions, especially on house training? Seems like all I do is yell at him.

A: Crate train your pup; (he will seldom mess his bed) and when you let him out of the crate, immediately carry him outside. A pup can usually "hold it" for one hour per month of age. Praise him when he "goes" outside. Yelling after the fact falls on deaf puppy ears since he can't connect your rage with something that happened mere minutes ago. Exercise him, encourage him to go before coming into the crate. Take him outside before crating him, every time.

Q: What are the best and worst names for bird dogs you have ever heard?

A: "Cricket" was just right for a nimble shorthair we just hunted with. "Flick" is a great spaniel name. I like any dog name that is earned, or has a great story behind it, such as "Three Devil's Yankee's Buddy." As for worst, it's quite common. Many young dogs share the first name "Dammit."

Valley quail habitat: folds in terrain, thick cover, clear ground under that cover.

Q: How valuable do you believe electronic training collars are to your dog-training program?

A: Very valuable. I love those hundred-yard check cords! If you believe that you should never give a command you can't enforce, an electronic collar gives you more control of your dog. But they are easily misused, so watch the accompanying DVD, consult with pro trainers, and ask lots of questions. Keep the voltage as low as possible—electronic "stimulation" is not about punishment as much as being about interrupting a dog's train of thought before he commits an infraction.

Q: I am looking for a good pointer for quail and pheasant hunting. I travel quite a bit for work so I also want the dog to keep my wife company when I am gone. Any suggestions on a breed?

A: Pointing breeds need a lot of training. All dogs need human interaction. Even as they mature they need refresher training if you want them to remain steady. Many are also one-man dogs. Get a flushing breed and you and your wife will both be happier.

Q: Do beeper collars ruin a dog's hearing?

A: I've never seen any evidence of this; however, a shotgun muzzle blast can adversely affect a dog. Avoid shooting directly over your dog whenever possible.

Q: Can any dog be trained for hunting or are there only certain breeds that work well? Does age matter when training a dog or is it true that you can't teach an old dog new tricks?

A: I've taught old dogs new tricks. It's fun for both parties. Certain breeds work better than others, but anything is possible. I've seen border collies, poodles, and German shepherd dogs in the field as well as some miraculous farm mutts.

You'll have better luck with a breed that evolved and was developed to utilize its scenting, pointing, flushing, and retrieving instincts.

Q: Recently, my dad and I have started to get more into upland game hunting. I have been looking at a variety of dogs and trying to figure out which breed to get and from which kennel. Everyone has their opinions in online forums. My wife and I are just starting our family, so we are anxious to get a dog that will be good around babies, but that will also perform well in the field. What should I get and from where?

A: A new baby will be taking most of your time. Personally, I would wait until you've got the child-rearing thing under control. A pup is a big responsibility, too, so somebody will get the short end of the stick. When you've figured out child-rearing, get a flushing breed that comes from family-friendly lines to maximize your enjoyment of the dog and the kid.

Q: How do you tell your buddy his dog sucks?

A: Careful, them's fightin' words. He will undoubtedly take it personally, especially if he disagrees with your assessment. Try offering to help with training, or buy him a book or video. Invite him over to watch *Wingshooting USA* to raise the bar a bit. Is his dog better than your dog? Why aren't you hunting with yours, then? If you don't have a dog, remember that beggars have a hard time being choosers.

Q: What do you find to be the best method to keep a flushing breed from breaking and running on the flush? My Lab goes after chukar and ends up running them or flushing them out of range.

A: Your dog is working too far ahead, out of gun range. As a flusher, he must be trained to stay close enough so you can shoot at what he flushes. Once you've got his range under control, spaniel trainers teach "Hup," stopping or sitting at the flush. A check cord and slow, gentle training of this obedience skill is what you need. Is he a water dog too? Will he obey hand signals? If so, the long whistle that sits him to take a line will work.

Q: I worry about my dog getting too cold while out duck hunting even though she wears appropriate gear. What are the signs of hypothermia in dogs and what action should be taken to correct it?

A: Shivering that doesn't stop is probably a good sign. Stumbling or other signs of coordination loss are, too, as is lack of interest. An insulated vest is good insurance. If you sense your dog is getting seriously cold, get him out of the wind, get him dry, and wrap him in a sleeping bag or blanket. Put him in a warm truck and head for the vet!

Q: How can I get a normally close-working pointing dog not to jump birds when he gets to a wide-open expanse of corn or hay? He is terrific in moderate to heavy cover but when released in a wide-open field he runs around like a nut. I want to correct him but not when he is so driven and bird oriented.

A: I recently lived your situation in South Dakota with my young wirehair Manny. One of the challenges with big country, especially a row crop like corn, is that birds will use the rows as freeways—running as far as they can since there's nothing to stop them. Simple solution: use a close-working flusher. Harder solution: more steadiness training so a running bird won't entice the dog to chase. Some pointing-breed trainers will condition their dogs to track a running bird, but slowly, so the gunners can catch up and shoot the bird when it finally does fly.

Q: I am very interested in hunting birds with my son, but we do not know any people who hunt. We are looking to find a place for us to spend time together and enjoy a nice day of hunting.

A: You get extra kibble just for thinking of doing such a great lifelong favor for your son! Watch my show together for a distilled version of the best parts of a hunt and the dogs we love. Seek out a local chapter of Pheasants Forever or other wildlife groups and join them. If there is a hunting dog club in your area, join it, even if you don't have a dog. Help others with training and projects and I'll wager you'll be invited on a hunt. Take a few shooting lessons together from a certified instructor who also hunts. Or, go to a local shooting preserve (which will supply guns, dogs, guides, and birds) for a half- or full-day hunt.

Q: I have a Large Munsterlander that will point but not consistently. He kind of hunts for himself. He is almost five years old and I'm not available to train him as much as I'd like. Is he too old to take to a trainer at this point for finishing?

A: Take him, but be there to be trained yourself. Training is not a one-time-only project, especially with a pointing breed. Your Large needs regular attention … "tuning up" … and plenty of bird contact, to become a better hunter. His age is not the issue. Your time commitment and willingness to regularly reinforce what any trainer first does is the critical factor.

Q: How can I break my dog from pointing songbirds while hunting? He is an English setter. Is that normal behavior for a hunting dog?

A: Perfectly normal, especially for a young dog. How many game birds does he get to point? That will help him learn the difference between tweety birds and the real deal. I wouldn't discourage a young dog from pointing anything. Pups will point butterflies, fire hydrants, and virtually anything that surprises them. What you need to do is give your setter a regular opportunity to sniff game birds. He'll learn what is expected from your praise for finding the right game, and not stinky birds or garden gnomes.

Q: Scott, I love the dogs with which you hunt. I was wondering about the range of the wirehairs. I need a dog that covers more ground than my short-hair. That way the wide-running dog would complement the close dog.

A: Before you make that investment, think about your close-working dogs. Are they close because they find birds close? In more open country, with sparser bird concentrations, do they range farther? If so, there's probably not a wirehair in your future. Mine will stretch out in sparse cover if the birds are scattered, but they'll also hunt close in the puckerbrush or when birds are thick. Wires are not typically big runners; in fact, your shorthairs may run bigger. If you want more range than that, maybe an English pointer is in your future.

Q: How suitable are Brittanys for quail hunting? Are they too energetic to halt and hold point?

A: Some of the best quail dogs in pro Rick Smith's string are Britts. Energetic is an asset; uncontrolled chaos is not. Like any pointing breed, a Brittany can be taught that he must find and point birds, holding steady until asked to move on or retrieve.

Classic sharptail grouse prairie. They'll be on the high spots.

Q: What are some methods to try with a dog that has a hard mouth or that is prone to chomping a bird on the retrieve (not eating the bird, just zealous death chomps)?

A: Usually, I'm content to get a bird back, period. "Zealous death chomp" is not only a great name for a heavy metal band but tolerated at times by this trainer. If it's not truly "hard mouth" resulting in torn-up or swallowed birds, try shooting straighter so all the birds are good and dead before your dog retrieves. (That's a little joke—I'm the last guy to be making suggestions like that.) But seriously, a live bird that flaps, flops, squawks, or scratches is a bummer for your dog; no wonder he wants to quiet it down. Practice with dead birds for a while. The ultimate solution, though, is force training—the entire retrieve becomes an obedience skill with no tolerance for chomping.

Q: What is the best way to break a dog from jumping into the air to catch a bird on the flush?

A: If it's a pointing breed, go back to steadiness training and "Whoa." If it's a flushing breed, give him a dog biscuit for his spirit. Then, teach "Hup," with verbal and whistle commands. The dog should sit on the flush or command, or the shot, and not retrieve until commanded to do so. No matter the breed or the weight of your game bag, never shoot low birds; one mistake is all it takes.

Q: I am an older hunter and am interested in getting a calmer-bred upland bird dog. Which one would you recommend?

A: Some of the versatile breeds may be just what the veterinarian ordered. "Ugly dogs" like the Spinone Italiano or Wirehaired Pointing Griffons generally hunt closer and slower than other breeds. The Clumber Spaniel is like a springer in slow motion. Or, a field-bred cocker spaniel will hunt close because with their short legs they can't get up much speed!

Q: Scott, how and what have you found to help with the passing of one of your own dogs after they have celebrated their hunting career with you?

A: This one is tough and I'm sorry if you lost a dog recently. I'll never get over the companionship, hard work, and loyalty my dogs showed me. That's the principal reason I make my TV show. To show my gratitude and respect, I wear my dogs' collar tags on my whistle lanyard. I know someone who puts their dogs' collars under the driver's seat of their truck. Paintings, impressions of paw prints . . . you'll find something that reminds you of the good times you had hunting with them. Reminiscing over a cold beer is always effective.

Q: How can you energize a young dog that seems lethargic when yard training? My six-month-old wirehaired Vizsla has all the energy in the world in the field but when training in the yard he tends to have a lot of quit in him.

A: Usually, yard work is boooooooring to a dog. Remember your worst job? It's why they gave you money to do it. Offer praise, treats, or whatever reward serves as your dog's "paycheck." Yard training is especially dull if it moves slowly, with little challenge or progression in skill level. It gets worse when birds aren't part of the equation. Introduce birds (live or dead) and I bet he'll perk up. Be methodical in how you progress from basic skills to more advanced work, but keep it moving forward, even if you experience setbacks periodically. Raise the bar, challenge your dog regularly, and make it fun.

Q: I have a one-year-old Lab. She is very smart and well behaved until we have guests. She will jump up, bark, and whine—totally out of character. What are some ways of correcting this behavior?

A: At least you didn't mention crotch sniffing! Short answer: gradual conditioning using baby steps. Identify and eliminate triggers (doorbell, for example). Teach obedience: sit, stay, quiet. Keep the energy level low. Put some distance between the dog and the guest, working closer and closer as the dog remains calm and on task with the command. Be ready to correct—i.e., praise—when she obeys, and move guest and dog closer together over many practice sessions. I've found that yelling doesn't help—it actually can raise the excitement level and things then spiral out of control faster.

Q: Do you typically recommend pet insurance for a hunting dog?

A: I've looked at this question frequently (usually after an expensive vet visit), and if you have ready access to cash, the short answer is no. If you can't afford an expensive emergency but can afford a monthly premium, invest in it. One consumer magazine I read studied the question and found it seldom pencils out as a good investment in the long run.

Q: What breeds are most suitable for pointing, flushing, and retrieving and will still make a good house dog that is suitable for small children?

A: That's a tall order. A pointer doesn't usually get to flush. A flusher won't point. Choose one or the other. Labs and golden retrievers are easy keepers and good family dogs but many haven't seen a game bird in several generations. The versatile breeds have many of the same family-friendly traits and will point. Smaller dogs like spaniels from good breeders may be your choice if the kids are really young. Just make sure the children are trained to respect and be careful around the dog.

Q: My golden retriever loves pheasant and quail hunting. She is nearly seven years old and doesn't hold a point longer than ten seconds. At this advanced age can she be trained to hold a point?

Low-growing sage like this is where you'll find
sage grouse.

A: Goldens are flushing retrievers, not pointers. That she points at all is impressive, but it's not her job. Instead, she should be encouraged to charge in hard to get a bird in the air for the gun, then hold still or sit to watch the shot bird fall. You're working against genetics to expect a retriever to be a pointer.

Q: In your personal experience, which breed of bird dog is the easiest to train, starting the dog as a puppy?

A: They're all a challenge, especially if you want a well-rounded and good-natured, obedient dog. A flushing dog can be hunting well in its first season if the dog will come on command. Pointing dogs require much more work to be steady to a flush, shot, and fall.

Q: Your thoughts on airline travel with your four-legged hunting companion? I know you drive to most of your locations but what has your experience been with air travel, if any? I would like to take my Boykin to South Dakota to hunt pheasants this fall but am not sure about the trip: two flight legs and a long day in the crate without having access to her.

A: I've never put a dog on an airplane so I can't speak from experience. But, that's telling in itself. Practically speaking, many airlines won't fly a dog if the weather is too cold or too warm. If they will take your dog, two flights mean you're trusting baggage handlers to do the right thing four different times—put her on, off, on, and off without blowing it. It's a risk I prefer not to take.

Q: I am working with two English pointers: a two-year-old male that is a natural and a three-year-old female with some issues. If both dogs are working the field together the male takes the lead and the female tends to sit back and not hunt. In addition, when the female is hunting with the male she is very aggressive toward the birds and tends to not hold point. Is there a way to train them to hunt together? Will the female learn from the male?

A: I'd hunt them separately—maybe forever. The female will learn from the male, acquiring both good and bad habits. She will never be bold and independent if she continues to let the male do the heavy lifting. And as you've learned, she has a competitive streak that causes her to break point. That probably isn't doing the male any good either. He might start busting birds too. Save yourself some anxiety and hunt them one at a time.

Q: What is proper etiquette when hunting your dog with someone else's dog for the first time?

A: Most of the time, everyone is happier when you hunt dogs singly. Alternate them, then compare and contrast their styles at the end of the day over a tall, cold one. Dogs need to be trained to hunt as a brace, must honor each other's points and retrieves, and obviously need to get along. If you must hunt them at the same time, try spreading out—way out—effectively hunting by yourselves. If that doesn't discourage you, introduce the dogs on neutral ground with leashes loose so they are not feeling your stress, and if possible hunt dogs of opposite sex together.

Q: What are the pros and cons of a pointer versus a flushing dog?

A: Both have their advantages and disadvantages. A flusher will probably be ready to perform reliably a season sooner than a pointer, because you don't have to work on steadying the dog while on point. But if you are dazzled by a staunch point, you'll be willing to wait a season. On the other hand, few feelings match the constant adrenaline flow of following a close-working flusher. Both need training to retrieve reliably.

Q: I have a ten-month old German shorthaired pointer that has a lot of energy. We don't have a good offseason place to train. What are some good tips for yard training that would not promote bad habits?

A: The only thing you can't do in the yard that you can do in the field is extend the distance your dog covers to perform his duties. I've found that yard-training problems start when skilled dogs get bored. Too much repetition is often the problem. How about developing a regimen of several skills and rotate through them at a relatively fast pace, like the weight training we do at the gym? A couple of repetitions for each skill are plenty in any session. Challenge the dog by going a little beyond his comfort zone for each skill. That said, find a way to give your dog hard exercise at least every other day to avoid obedience problems. Hitching him to a bike or jogging on a leash are better than nothing.

Q: How do you keep the burrs from building up on long-haired dogs?

A: Burrs are a fact of hunting life, but luckily, my dogs aren't as long haired as some! A good comb-out is all it takes for my wirehairs, and they get that at the end of the day, along with a thorough check of eyes, ears, toes, and bellies, to make sure there are no seeds, cuts, scrapes, or bugs. Longer-haired dogs will need more of the same, or a good haircut prior to the season. Some owners use ShowSheen, a horse product that makes most stuff slide off long hair quite easily.

Q: How do you teach your pointer not to bump or get too close when pointing?

A: Two separate challenges, two solutions. Once a dog knows what birds smell like, you need to insist that he stop immediately upon sniffing one. Walking him into the scent cone while on a check cord and stopping him upon his first indication of smelling birds will help him point farther from the birds. With a remote-controlled launcher, you can fly birds if he tries to sneak in after scenting them. Steadiness—not bumping once he's on point—is an obedience skill. When a dog indicates he's found a bird by pointing, your job starts. Through any number of signals, you need to teach him that he should stand still—"Whoa"—until you tell him to move again to retrieve, hunt on, or heel.

Q: At what age should you introduce live birds to a pup?

A: Early, in controlled situations, so he can't get scared or injured by flapping wings or claws. Lately, though, I'm becoming a believer in the old-school strategy. When your pup demonstrates interest in birds, work on pointing and steadiness, obedience, and possibly retrieving. You avoid the biggest banes of pointing dog owners: dogs that chase flying birds into the next time zone, and breaking on the flush. While birds are a great motivator and reward for dogs, they probably shouldn't be the reason he holds once he hits a point. That's an obedience skill.

Q: I have a ten-month-old German shorthair that hunts well. How do I get her to stop stealing other dogs' retrieves?

A: Yard work. A retrieve and bird-in-mouth shouldn't be the natural result of every point (or flush, for spaniels). In training, it should be a rare treat, with the handler picking up most of the birds. This breaks the chain of expectation inherent in the sequence of find-point-flush-break-retrieve. Once your dog learns that not every flushed bird is hers, introduce other dogs and make her

Typical South Dakota pheasant hunt about to get underway.

remain steady while they retrieve. Again, it's an obedience challenge.

Q: I just started upland hunting last year in Colorado with my German shorthaired pointer and was wondering what advice you can offer about dealing with rattlesnake bites. We haven't had any run-ins yet but I've seen quite a few while out scouting the areas we plan on hunting this year.

A: My strategy includes snake-aversion sessions (only with a pro), and carrying an antihistamine like Benadryl. If your dog gets bit, open the Benadryl capsule and pour the powder under his tongue, holding his mouth shut until it dissolves. Keep the dog as quiet as possible, carry him to your truck, and hightail it to the nearest veterinarian for observation and treatment. If your area is particularly snake prone, wait until the weather is cold to start your season, after most snakes will be denned up for winter. Just be careful during unusual winter thaws. The new vaccine holds promise, but only works on some types of rattlesnakes.

Q: My Lab becomes a bit wild when she doesn't get out to exercise. Any suggestions for when you want to try and train her but she is just too wild?

A: Many guys joke about letting their dog out of the truck five miles before a hunt or training session so it has time to settle down—and in some cases it's not a joke! But, you won't always have that opportunity, so your dog must learn that work is work. Get back to obedience basics, and add some clear signals that it's time for learning, not playing. Put the dog up on the training table or clip the leash on, for example. Keep your energy level down, set a vocal tone that's all business. Start each session with some fundamental obedience skills to set the mood.

Q: I have a female German shorthair that is six years old. I feed premium food but cannot keep weight on her when hunting season begins. I've tried satin balls, canned food, soft food, etc., in addition to her dry food, but she always loses weight. She is healthy and happy and has energy but I worry about her being so skinny. What can I do?

A: I've got a young wirehair with the same problem, and many of the same solutions have been tried at my house. First, check with your veterinarian to make sure it's not a medical issue and she really is underweight. Then, shop for a higher-protein and higher-fat food, likely without grain. Many trainers add fat to dry food, such as butter, coconut, or olive oil. There are also powdered versions available. Try www.elements-nutrition.com for more products that might help.

Q: Where do you start in finding a good bird dog for purchase?

A: Buy some gun dog magazines and study the ads and articles. Join a club and attend meetings and training sessions where you can get to know local owners and breeders. Ask them where they get their dogs. Attend hunt tests and meet breeder-trainers. Most national groups have a database of hunt test results—another great source—showing you which dogs (potential parents of your new dog) and breeders are excelling in the field. When you observe a great dog in action, ask the owner how you can get one too.

Q: Scott, my dogs have only hunted and trained with quail. Will they point other upland birds such as grouse and Hungarian partridges? I want to take a trip out west, but don't know if they will perform as well as they do here in the South.

A: They'll probably do just fine. I've never seen any science on this, but I believe a gun dog reacts to the volume of scent (bigger bird, more scent?) and so will recognize similarities in the scent of Huns or grouse. I'd pay money to see his face when one of those gigantic "quail" flushes in front of him!

Q: We have a German shorthair that gets sore paws but will not hunt with boots on. Any tips?

A: Try duct tape instead of boots—instructions elsewhere in this book or on my website. Tape or boots, most dogs get used to them pretty fast, but I'd still practice at home before a hunt.

Find ruffed grouse among the tangles.

Q: What length of check cord is most appropriate for a vizsla pup?

A: Twenty to thirty feet should be plenty.

Q: We have five German shorthairs. Our two boys (fourteen and nine) love helping to train them. Any suggestions or techniques that will encourage them to keep doing this? We do not use any force break training, just positive reinforcement techniques.

A: Take them all hunting. While training can be a lot of fun, at some point you must introduce them to live birds. Hunt tests or field trials are good "final exams" for your training assistants.

Q: Is it better to let kids use lighter adult guns or should I try tracking down a youth gun?

A: It's not so much weight as gun fit. A shorter stock will be best for smaller hunters because it will come up to their shoulder more smoothly, create the proper sight picture, and lead to more successful shooting. Eventually, they will grow into adult-sized shotguns, so start saving now!

Q: I hunted as a kid with my father, back when it was free. Our dog Buster was from my grandfather's old matriarch, Queenie, and the quail were wild, fast, and small, but tasty. Can it still be enjoyed as much as it was back then?

A: Yes. You might have to drive farther or pay a bit, but it sounds like you already know why those are minor inconveniences.

Q: I have a German wirehair puppy that loves water. She runs down to the lake every chance she gets. Splashes around, drinks her fill, wades into her chest, but will not swim. I have tossed bumpers, balls, and toys etc., but she just jumps around and barks.

A: Keep trying. Try real birds and eventually she will become one motivated swimmer.

Q: At what age is it the best time to spay or neuter your dog?

A: Most research suggests you wait anywhere from six months to eighteen months to ensure that the hormones "down there" have a chance to work their magic on the dog's body.

Q: What is the best method to convince your children not to undo your dog's training? Every bit of progress seems to be undone, for instance, by the kid's uncontrollable urge to play tug-of-war with the dog, etc.

A: Train your kids too. Get them to help with and understand your training and it might have more relevance to them.

Q: Is it easier for a dog to understand two commands ("Sit" and "Stay") or is it easier to teach a single command?

A: I like to keep it simple. A dog should obey the command until released or given another command. When he "Sits," he sits until told to do something else.

Look for Gambel's quail in desert country like this.

Q: Scott, I live in the big city and own a young German shorthair. What do you think is the best way for me to keep my dog in shape for hunting? Not only physically but also her bird-finding skills?

A: Running alongside your bike (attached via a rig like the Springer) would be good for physical conditioning. Even a small backyard can be used for fundamental bird contact, especially combined with a long drive once a week to a spot where you can let your dog stretch out and find birds in a more natural setting.

Q: Is it okay to "roughhouse" with my dog while playing with him or does that affect his discipline?

A: I do it occasionally, but not as often as I used to. I'm becoming a believer in "pecking order," and that requires discipline on the human's part as well as the dog's. A dog that learns he can "play fight" with you is one step away from jockeying for the position of top dog.

Q: What are your thoughts on hybrid breeds? I have hunted with a lodge that breeds the German shorthair with Labs. The result is a leaner, faster retriever and one that will point and/or flush wild pheasants. I was hesitant to obtain one of the pups until I worked with one last season.

A: I guess if you want a dog that flushes sometimes and points other times that would be the dog for you. I prefer a dog that I can count on to do one or the other consistently.

Q: Do dogs stay on the scent of a bird better when their nose is wet?

A: Great observation. I think so. More humidity, period, helps a dog scent better (scent molecules "stick" better to vegetation and the ground). A nose that is damp collects more scent. Nostrils (where dogs' scent receptors are) that are damp are able to use more of those receptors.

Q: Is there a quality dog food that helps to limit the shedding of hair and the amount of gas that the dogs produce?

A: On the shedding question, probably not. See a veterinarian to make sure it's not a medical condition such as a thyroid imbalance. On the gas question, yes. Causes are often: a) overfeeding any ration; b) too much fat; c) too much protein; or d) a protein source that your dog is not able to metabolize well. Check your dog food's nutritional content and adjust one or more of those variables.

Q: I don't understand how you know when to shoot when the bird is far enough away after the dog flushes it. I have a feeling the dog is going to get hurt (shot).

A: Congratulations on having some awareness of the dog when shooting! As far as height, the general rule is never shoot at a bird unless you can see sky below the bird. As far as distance, only practice will make you comfortable with knowing "shootable" distances of fifteen to thirty-five yards. Luckily, the only way to do this is go hunting more often.

Q: I noticed while watching the show that you place a piece of tape on the left eye of your shooting glasses. I believe it's because your left eye is dominant and you shoot right-handed. So here is my question: Why don't you learn to shoot left-handed?

A: I've tried, and failed. Twice. The tape is not a perfect solution, but I don't mind missing birds (as you have probably observed on the show).

Your mother doesn't live here—pick up your empties.

Q: I have two Brittanys, full brothers from the same litter. One will almost always lie down when backing and stand when first to point, until I'm standing beside him. Then he may lie down. Sometimes it's not pretty, but it doesn't bother me too much as I just hunt and do not field trial. Are there any suggestions on correcting this? He is a little timid when corrected very much, but he is a hard hunter.

A: You've probably identified part of the problem. He's a soft dog that fears harsh correction. Maybe you came down hard on him a few times when he wasn't steady on a bird? Maybe instead of correcting him for flushing a bird, work on praising him when he "Whoas" for the same bird. He may come around if he's feeling good about the work he does for you.

12

The Ultimate Upland Checklist

"A dog is not 'almost human' and I know of no greater insult to the canine race than to describe it as such."

—John Holmes

IF YOU'VE EVER forgotten ammo, sleeping bag, or dog (yep, I've done all three) on a hunting trip, this list is dedicated to you. NASA doesn't launch a space shuttle without a check list, nor should you start a hunt without the confidence that comes from knowing you have all the necessary gear.

Thanks to all my viewers, blog subscribers, and seminar attendees who have helped add to this list over the years. While you may not need all of this stuff on every trip, some of it will come in handy on most trips—unless you forget it. From the feedback I've gotten, the only item not on the list that you might need is the semitruck to haul it all!

I try to keep this list updated at my blog: www.scottlindenoutdoors.com. It's a free download, so check in periodically, print it out, and keep it handy.

Dog Gear

Food
Bowl
Nutri-Cal or supplement bars

Electronic collar, charger, transmitter
Check cord
Whistle (and a spare)
Lead-leash
Crate
Maltodextrin supplement
Tie-out stake/cable
Microchip
Spare collar ID tag
Bell for collar
Skid plate/belly-protector
Vitamin C
Brush or comb (for removing burrs, tangles)
"Lost" kit (chip number, photo, license number) and preprinted flyers
Boots (or duct tape)
Food supplements to encourage eating at night
Extra collar
First aid kit plus:
    Eye-wash/saline solution
    Aspirin
    Ophthalmic antibiotic ointment
    De-skunking kit
    Hydrogen peroxide, dropper or squeeze bulb
    Bandages/gauze
    Vet wrap
    Superglue (nail repair)
    Dermabond
    Antihistamine (for snake/bee encounters)
    Pad Tuff
    EMT Gel
    Hemostats or tweezers
    Tick removal tool
Insect repellent spray/drops
List of veterinarians in area
Poop scooper or bags
Blaze-orange bandanna or vest
Veterinary-health certificates
Bumpers, toys
Nail clipper

Camp Gear

Bungee cords
Duct tape
Propane or white gas
Lawn chairs
Folding table
Ice chest
Trash bags
Ziplock food bags
Lantern, extra mantles
Hand axe
Water
Rope
Flashlight, extra batteries
Sleeping bag
Cot or sleeping pad
Pillow
Tent/vapor barrier, rain fly
Tent stakes, rope, poles
Insect repellent (human)
Shovel
Cooking gear
Cook stove
Paper towels
Tarp
Toilet paper
Repair kit: sleeping bag, air mattress, etc.

RV-Trailer-Camper Gear

Fill propane tank
Fill water tank
Charge batteries
Keys and spares
Wheel chocks and leveling blocks
Tire pressure gauge
Water hose
Drain hose
Power cable

Hunting Gear

Shotgun
Extra shotgun, same gauge
Ammo (including nontoxic)
Choke tubes
Hard gun case
Soft gun case or sock
Gun cleaning kit
Gun permits (Canada)
Choke tube wrench
Snap caps
Shooting gloves
GPS, spare batteries
Vest
Water bladder/bota
Hunter Education certificate (or previous license)
Contact information, itinerary to reliable person
Topo maps
Diary/journal
Landowner/host gifts
Shooting glasses
Regulation booklets
Hearing protection
Licenses/tags/permits
Extra car key
Game shears
Ten essentials survival kit:
    Duct tape
    Map and compass
    Waterproof matches
    Alternate fire starter
    Space blanket
    Aluminum foil
    Water purification (tabs or filter)
    Water container
    Whistle
    Multi-tool
Ziplock bags for bird storage
Flashlight/headlamp

Sunblock
SPOT messenger/PLB
Towel/chamois

Personal Gear

Medications, vitamins
First aid kit
Boot dryer
Cell phone, charger
Laptop, charger
Still camera, memory cards, USB cable
Video camera, tripod, batteries, tape or disks
Wallet, cards, and cash
Reading glasses
Sunglasses
Toilet paper
Toiletries, toothbrush, etc.

Transportation Gear

Jerry cans with extra fuel
Two-way radios, batteries
Spare serpentine belt
Air compressor
Antifreeze
Books on tape or music CDs
Windshield wiper fluid
Hi-Lift jack
Shovel
Come-along or winch
Road maps
Spare key
Jumper cables
Tow strap
Tool kit
Tire sealant
Fire extinguisher
Ice scraper
Spare fuses

Spare bulbs
Lug wrench
Tire chains
GPS
Jumpstarter/power source
Check all fluid levels

Clothing

Rain/wind pants, jacket
Wicking underwear
Brush chaps
Socks, liner
Socks, wool blend
Bandanna
Insulating layer (fleece)
Hat or cap, plus spares
Shirts
Pants
Street shoes
Sleepwear
Gloves
Boot repair goo
Boots, two pairs
Blaze orange as required by law
Belt
Chemical hand warmers

13

Glossary of Bird Dog Terms

"The average dog is a nicer person than the average person."

—Andy Rooney

EVERY PASSION HAS a lexicon. It's one way to ensure clear communication, but it also tends to exclude outsiders, newcomers, or competitors. I don't buy the latter rationale. Instead, let's level the linguistic playing field and help everyone enjoy our sport, our dogs, and the wild places we love:

AA: All Age dog, as defined by AKC. Competes in All Age stakes, which are open to a dog of any age.

AFC: Amateur Field Champion.

AKC: American Kennel Club.

AI: Artificial insemination.

Air washed: A bird that has recently flown and landed and thus has yet to leave much scent where it landed.

All Age Stake: Field trial competition open to all dogs of a specified breed or breeds without restriction as to the age of the dog, but which may be restricted by other conditions that are deemed necessary by the organizing club.

Alter: To spay or neuter a dog. Also "fix."

American Field: Sporting dog association that tests and registers pointing dogs; publishes *The Field Dog Stud Book*.

Automatic, semiautomatic: Shotgun with a magazine designed to hold extra shells and is reloaded by a mechanical process activated by the recoil of the shot (or a gas piston) and can fire another round with each trigger pull.

Avoidance training: Using voice, physical, or electric training collar to dissuade a dog from certain behaviors, i.e., approaching snakes.

Back: Dog stopping upon encountering another dog's point.

Barrel: Lying on its side, it is often used to teach steadiness by placing the dog on the uneven, slippery, or unsteady rounded side.

Biddable: Willing to take direction, easy to train.

Blind: 1) "Blind retrieve" is one where the dog did not see the bird or dummy fall and must be directed by the handler with hand, whistle, or verbal directions; 2) Brush pile or other structure designed to conceal waterfowl hunters.

Blinking: Briefly pointing a bird and then leaving it, or upon finding a bird avoiding retrieving it, or purposely avoiding a bird after catching scent.

Bob: Bobwhite quail.

Bore: Shotgun muzzle measurement, often stated as "gauge" except for .410 caliber.

Brace: 1) Two dogs hunting the same area, often in field trial or hunt tests; 2) Pair of shot birds.

Breakaway: A brace of dogs released simultaneously to begin a field trial run, usually commanded by the judge.

Broke dog: Steady to flush and will honor a bracemate's point (back). Other definitions extend to steady-to-fall or include retrieving.

Bumper: A retrieving training device, often tubular in shape and made of canvas or plastic.

Bust: To flush a bird or covey, usually done inadvertently by the dog.

Bye dog: A dog braced with another dog competing in a hunt test or field trial but not being judged. Used to ensure fairness as each dog must hunt at least part of the event with another dog.

Call back: At a field trial, high-placing dogs are offered a "call back" to continue competition after other dogs have been eliminated.

Campaign: To participate in a number of field trials in pursuit of a title.

Carding: Attaching a piece of cardboard to a bird's leg with a cord in order to slow down or shorten its flight. Used in training steadiness.

CERF: Canine Eye Registry Foundation. Evaluates breeding dogs for hereditary eye defects.

Chain gang: A long ground-level chain attached to two stakes with dogs attached via short chain at intervals between the stakes.

Check cord: Long rope or similar item attached to a dog's collar and used to direct or correct it.

Command lead: Developed by pro trainer Delmar Smith, a lariat-type rigid rope-slip collar used to teach obedience and hunting commands by exerting gentle pressure on the dog's neck.

Cover: Crops, brush, or other vegetation harboring game birds.

Cover dog: Any dog that commonly hunts heavy "cover" (forested, brushy habitat) for a hunter on foot. Historically applied to grouse and woodcock dogs and habitat, now expanding to virtually any dense vegetation and any breed that is used to hunt in it.

Cover: Act of a dog breeding a bitch.

Covert: 1) A likely bird-harboring spot; often in a woods or forest; also sometimes "cover."

Covey: Group of birds, often a family or brood.

Crate: Box, cage, or similar device to transport or house a dog.

Cross dominance: A condition where a shooter's "off" eye is stronger than the one sighting down the shotgun barrel.

Derby Stake: Field trial competition for dogs between six months of age and two years of age.

Deutsch Langhaar: German longhaired pointer.

DKV: Deutsch Kurzhaar Verband, German-based shorthair club.

Ditch parrot: Colloquial term for ring-necked pheasant.

Diversion: In retriever tests and trials, a person, shot, or bird that distracts the dog from his assigned tasks; used to test the dog's level of training.

Dock: To cut a dog's tail to less-than-natural length.

Double: 1) Two birds that flush simultaneously; 2) Side-by-side or over-under shotgun; 3) Act of shooting two birds or clay targets.

Drilling: German term for a gun that has three barrels, usually one rifled barrel under two shotgun barrels.

Dummy: Another term for bumper, a retrieving training device usually tubular in shape and made of plastic or canvas.

Fall: Shot bird that has dropped to the ground.

FC: AKC title, Field Champion.

Field Dog Stud Book (FDSB): A document published by the American Field Publishing Company in Chicago, registering many field-trial breeds, including setters and pointers.

Field trial: A competition in which dogs are judged on ability and style in tracking, finding, coursing, or retrieving game.

Fix: Spay or neuter a dog. Also "alter."

Flank: The part of a dog's body immediately forward of his back leg.

Flight pen: An enclosure made of netting where birds are raised or held before being planted at a hunting preserve.

Flush: 1) Act of a bird taking flight; 2) Act of a dog or person forcing the bird to fly.

Force train, force break: Training to retrieve through any number of methods using an ear pinch, toe pinch, or similar physical force.

Furnishings: Hair, eyebrows and whiskers, tail hair. In some breeds, furnishings must meet specific criteria for length or texture.

Futurity: A non-regular competition at field trials for young dogs that requires a series of nominations and associated fees prior to the date on which the Futurity is judged. These stages usually consist of nomination of the bitch after she is bred, nomination of the litter after it is whelped, and/or nomination of individual puppies from the litter.

Gauge: Size of a shotgun barrel's diameter at the muzzle end (excepting .410 caliber).

Get: Offspring.

Green broke: Often the same as a "started" dog. Indicates some level of training in obedience and elementary hunting skills, usually including pointing.

GMHR: Grand Master Hunting Retriever. An NAHRA title.

GRHRCH: Grand Hunting Retriever Champion. A UKC/HRC title denoting that a retriever has qualified in the annual HRC Grand event.

Gunner: 1) A hunter; 2) Term to describe designated shooters in a field trial.

Hack: To overhandle a dog, usually with a numerous unnecessary verbal or whistle commands.

Handler: The human who is hunting, training, or otherwise working a dog.

Hard mouth: A dog that squeezes or bites down on retrieved birds.

"Heel": Command word (and verb) when a dog walks alongside its handler "at heel," with its head no farther forward than your knee.

"Hie on": A command to urge the dog on, start, or resume hunting. Used in hunting or in field trials.

Hock: On a dog's body, the back leg's "knee."

Honor: 1) Stopping upon seeing another dog on point. Also "backing"; 2) Standing or sitting still while another dog retrieves a shot bird or dummy.

HR: Hunting Retriever, a UKC title.

Hun: Hungarian partridge.

"Hunt dead": Command given to a dog to search a general area for a shot bird rather than giving him a straight line to the point where the bird was known to have landed.

HRC: Hunting Retriever Club.

Hunting tests: Noncompetitive field events for flushing breeds, retrieving breeds, and pointing breeds, where dogs are evaluated against a standard rather than ranked against other dogs as in a field trial.

"Hup": Stop and sit at flush or upon command.

Instinctive: Shooting style where the shooter quickly mounts the shotgun and shoots, trusting hand-eye coordination to place the shot string into the bird's trajectory (rather than using lead, pull-through, or other methods).

Intact: Not spayed or neutered.

Jip: Female dog. Also "gyp"; often refers to an unbred female among houndsmen.

JGHV: Jagdgebrauchshundverband e.V., the umbrella organization of all versatile hunting dog clubs in Germany.

JS: Junior Hunter, title conferred on dogs that have qualified the required number of times in Junior tests at AKC hunting tests for spaniels, retrievers, and pointing breeds.

Kennel: 1) Dog boarding or training facility; 2) Dog box or cage for transport or sleeping.

Lead: In shooting, moving the shotgun muzzle to place the shot string ahead of the bird, anticipating its direction of flight.

Line: The starting point for tests, trials, and training.

Line manners: A term used to describe how a dog acts while sitting at the "line" under judgment.

Litter: The puppies of one whelping.

LM: Large Munsterlander, a versatile hunting breed.

Mark: 1) An item a dog sees thrown for it to retrieve. Usually a game bird or a training bumper; 2) The act of watching the item as it is thrown.

MH: Master Hunter, AKC title for which a dog must receive qualifying scores at six licensed or member tests. If the dog has already received a Senior Hunter title (SH), the dog need only qualify five times.

Memory bird: Any item in a multiple mark situation, other than the last item, a dog has seen thrown for it to retrieve.

MHR: Master Hunting Retriever, an NAHRA title.

NA: Natural Ability, the NAVHDA test for dogs up to sixteen months of age.

NADKC: North American Deutsch Kurzhaar Club, affiliate of the Deutsch Kurzhaar Verband (DKV).

NAFC: National Amateur Field Champion, an AKC title.

NAHRA: North American Hunting Retriever Association.

NAFC: National Amateur Field Champion, a prefix title or designation conferred on a dog that has won the National Amateur Championship field trial for its breed.

NFC: National Field Champion, a prefix title or designation conferred on a dog that has won the National Championship field trial for its breed when handled by a professional trainer.

NAVHDA: North American Versatile Hunting Dog Association.

NAPBA: North American Pudelpointer Breeders Alliance, breed testing and training group.

Neuter: To castrate or spay.

Non–slip retriever: Term used in connection with off-lead retriever field trials. A dog that is steady to wing, shot, and fall and only retrieves when commanded.

Novice Stake: Field trial competition confined to dogs that have not gained the following awards: first through fourth place in a twenty-four dog Open Stake; first, second, or third award in a twelve dog Open Stake; or first award in an All Aged or Novice Stake. For spaniels, Novice Stakes are open to dogs that have not gained a first, second, or third in Open Stakes or first in an All Age or Novice Stake.

NSTRA: National Shoot to Retrieve Association.

Objective: Field trial and hunting term for obvious bird-holding area, usually a bush or other well-defined obstacle where birds have been placed.

Open Stake: Field trial competition in which the dogs have the opportunity to gain a qualification toward the title of Field Trial Champion (FC) and toward entry in the Championships or Champion Stake for its breed.

OFA: Orthopedic Foundation for Animals, developed and maintains a registry of hip dysplasia in dogs. Dogs with OFA numbers are rated and certified free of canine hip dysplasia.

"Over": Dog-handling term to command a dog to hunt to one side of a field or water to retrieve.

Over and under: A shotgun with two barrels aligned vertically; also called "superposed."

PennHIP: A method of evaluating hip dysplasia in dogs by calculating hip laxity; within-breed ratings are provided, permitting breeders to select dogs with the best hips for breeding future generations.

Picked up: Taken out of competition and removed from the field. In a field trial, a dog is "picked up" at the order of a judge.

Plant: Placing a bird on the ground, usually to provide game for a field trial or hunt test or training session.

Point: The intense, stylized stance of the hunting dog, taken to indicate the presence and position of game. Often includes a front leg and tail up.

Poison bird: A mark the dog must ignore to successfully complete the assigned task, usually a blind.

Prize: In the NAVHDA testing system, each level includes three "prizes," I, II, and III, indicating to what degree the dog accomplished each task in the test. Minimum scores in certain test areas are required to earn each prize level.

PPNA: Pudelpointer Club of North America, breed club.

Pull away: Style of shooting in which the shooter places the shotgun muzzle on the bird and then moves it forward to achieve lead.

Pump: Shotgun that is reloaded by sliding back the fore-end to eject the empty shell and move an unspent shell into the breech.

Puppy Stake: Field trial competition for dogs whelped no earlier than January 1 in the year preceding the date of the field trial. If a Puppy Stake is run in January then a dog that was a puppy in the previous year is still considered a puppy.

Quartering: A left–right–left pattern the dog runs in the field, generally in an arc in front of the hunter.

Race: A dog's performance style in terms of ground coverage and speed; i.e., a dog with big forward race is far in front of the handler and covering a lot of ground side-to-side as well.

Range: The distance a dog hunts from his handler.

Relocate: Resuming hunting on his own or upon command, after a dog has pointed a bird (that has apparently moved off).

Retired gun: Used in multiple marks, after an assistant has thrown the item to be retrieved, he or she moves to a concealed location so when the dog returns to the line and looks out to their mark, the assistant ("gun") is hidden from view.

Roading: Forcing a dog to pull against some form of weight (ATV, bike, horse, chain harnessed to the dog) to increase its strength and stamina.

Scout: Field trial assistant who rides horseback to help locate the dog for the handler.

SH: Senior Hunter, a suffix title conferred on dogs that have qualified the required number of times in Senior tests at hunting tests for pointing breeds, retrievers, and spaniels.

Service: Breeding, as when the male dog "services" a bitch.

Set: Lying down upon encountering birds. Historically, setter-type dogs did this before firearms became prevalent so a net-throwing hunter would have an unobstructed toss to the birds

Sharp: An aggressive dog is "sharp." In some breed clubs sharpness is desired for dogs that must dispatch vermin.

Shot size: Size of the pellets in a shotgun shell.

Shot string: Pellets as they leave the shotgun muzzle spread longitudinally as well as vertically. When the shot string arrives at the target some pellets may be several feet ahead of others.

Side by side: Shotgun with two barrels aligned horizontally.

Single: One bird.

Shuck: 1) Act of reloading a pump shotgun; 2) Spent shotgun shell, also called a "hull."

Singing: In field trials, handlers will shout or "sing" so their dog knows his location.

Skeet: American clay target game created to simulate bird hunting, usually featuring two towers from which targets are thrown as shooters move in a semicircular pattern from station to station.

SM: Small Munsterlander, a versatile hunting breed.

Soft: Sensitive to harsh training methods.

Soft mouth: If the birds a dog retrieves are undamaged, the dog has a "soft mouth."

Spaniel: Any of the dog breeds originally from Spain that flush birds rather than point them. Examples: springer spaniel, cocker spaniel.

Spinone Italiano: A versatile hunting breed.

Sporting Clays: A British clay target game originally envisioned so that targets would imitate hunting situations, thus its original name of "Hunter's Clays."

SR: Started Retriever. An NAHRA title

Stake: Designation of a class or separately judged competition in field trials.

Stand: To point a bird.

Started dog: A dog that is partially obedience trained, comes when called and will point birds. See "Green Broke."

Staunch: Holding still, usually in the presence of a bird, despite distraction or temptation. Sometimes refers to a more intense or stylish point.

Steady: Stable, not moving while on point or sitting (for retrievers or flushing breeds). Steady to wing usually indicates a dog will hold point until the bird is flushed. A dog that is steady to shot holds point until the hunter shoots. A dog that is steady to fall awaits a command before breaking point to retrieve or hunt on.

Stimulation: Application of electric shock via training collar.

Stop to flush: Stopping upon seeing or hearing a bird fly.

Straw: Container holding dog semen, which is either chilled or frozen for later use.

Style: Subjective term describing a dog's work in the field and upon finding birds.

Sustained lead: Style of shooting in which the shooter points the shotgun muzzle ahead of the bird, maintains that lead as he tracks the bird's flight, and shoots ahead of the bird's trajectory.

Swing: In shooting, moving the gun muzzle in the direction the bird is flying.

Tethering: Tying a cord to a bird used for training so it will fly some distance and then fall to the ground so the trainer can use it again. Often, trainers will attach the other end of the cord to a "pigeon pole."

Tie-out stake: A metal post in the ground to which a dog is attached via a chain.

Timberdoodle: Woodcock, also called mud bat, bogsucker, and woodsnipe.

Training table, "Whoa" table: A raised platform on which a dog is placed for training.

Trap: 1) Original clay target game in which shooters are arrayed in an arc behind a trap house, from which clay targets fly away from the shooters; 2) In some hunt tests or trials, when a dog catches the bird prior to the flush.

Trash: Game you don't want your dog pursuing, i.e., deer, raccoons, mice, etc.

UH: Upland Hunter, a UKC title.

UPT: Utility Preparatory Test, a NAVHDA test for dogs over sixteen months of age. Includes many of the components of the Utility Test, but in simpler forms.

UT: Utility Test, for more advanced dogs in the NAVHDA system.

VC: Versatile Champion. A dog that has passed the highest test level in the NAVHDA system. A dog is invited to participate in the group's invitational test after earning a Utility Test Prize I.

VDD: Verein Deutsch Drahthaar, or German Wirehair Club based in Germany with an affiliate (VDDNA) in the United States and Canada)

VDDNA: Verein Deutsch Drahthaar North America, branch of the German-based VDD.

Versatile dog: Any of the hunting breeds developed in Europe in the 1800s for middle-class hunters who needed one dog to point, retrieve on land and water; track furred, feathered, and wounded big game; as well as protect the family. Examples: German shorthair, Spinone, Weimaraner, Viszla.

VHDF: Versatile Hunting Dog Federation. A dog testing and training club in the United States focusing on the continental or European breeds.

Viszla: Shorthaired versatile breed from Hungary.

Wachtelhund: German spaniel originally bred to hunt quail.

Weimaraner: Shorthaired versatile breed from Germany.

"Whoa": Command word to stop a dog and have him remain motionless until commanded to move.

"Whoa" barrel: Metal or plastic barrel laid horizontally on the ground on which trainers place dogs to encourage steadiness to the "Whoa" command and to live birds.

"Whoa" post: Metal or wood post in the ground around which a check cord is looped to stop a dog's forward movement.

"Whoa" table: Another term for "training table"; typically a low platform trainers put a dog on to teach or enforce commands, often accompanied by the "Whoa" command.

Wild flush: Bird that flies before the hunter or dog intentionally flushes it.

WPGCA: Wirehaired Pointing Griffon Club of America.

WR: Working Retriever, an NAHRA title.

Yard work: The term used to describe any number of training drills conducted in and around the kennel area or "yard."

Notes